THE 28 DAY

HAPPY

CHALLENGE

HAPPINESS HABITS FOR YOUR DAILY LIFE

by TANISHKA

Best Selling Author of 'Sacred Union' and 'The Inner
Goddess Makeover'

Published by Star of Ishtar Publishing www.starofishtar.com

ISBN 978-0-9874263-4-5

DEDICATION

In a world obsessed with celebrities, this book
is dedicated to those often unsung heroes and
heroines who respond with human kindness to the
suffering of others

May all beings in all worlds be happy

CONTENTS

PRAISE FOR THE 28 DAY HAPPY CHALLENGE

'Thank you for motivating me, I have made a morning ritual out of your 28 day happiness challenge. ..I will continue on...just wanted to say thank you!' Tara Jane

'This experience has been so uplifting.' Shelley Styles

'Thank you so much for this challenge. I have implemented some changes already and I look forward to your book.' Wendy Houston

'I can't believe it's been 28 days already! Blessings to you as you write the book this experience has inspired!' Ellen Niemeier

'Blessings to you. Thank you for all the sharing of your knowledge and true caring and love for all people. Namaste.' Rosy McCain

'O wow!! Thank you so much for putting it all into action so beautifully! Amazing!! I found this experience with you, life changing. I want to do this 28 days again! Can you please ensure access to this info after the event? Thank you again!!!' Elizabeth Roux

'Thank you for taking the time to do this. Your messages always pop up just when needed. So very grateful!' Jay Kerr

'Thank you so much for sharing your insight and wisdom. I've looked forward to reading your messages each day, which were always in sync with areas I needed to grow from. Blessings and love to you.' Kylie Hudson

'Am gonna miss this inspiration every day. Thank-you so much.' Denise Gronert

'Thank you for sharing and caring about the heart of happiness and connecting with the authentic true self. Your 28 Day Happiness Challenge has been an inspiration and a blessing.' Caroline Georgieff

'I'm loving these posts!! Don't want the month to end!! Xx' Wendy Huntriss

'Your writings are so uniquely accurate ! Thank you for your tips'
Katharina Erol

'I'm loving these tips.' Julia King

'I've loved these daily posts - thank you!! Will definitely keep my eye out for the book' Michele Harrod

'Hi, is there a way I could save all this wonderful advice/tips to read over in the future??? thanks you in advance....and thank you for these words of wisdom x' Nicola Young.

THE INVITATION

Wouldn't you like to wake up smiling?

Imagine waking up as you did as a small child, happy to be alive and excited by what the day will bring!

We all start life this way...rising with the sun and beaming with JOY!

Then we encounter disappointments with the inevitable loss of innocence and it gets harder and harder to get up in the morning, with a smile on our face to greet the day.

So if you can read one suggestion a day, I can help you find your way back to that way of being. (Without substances.)

The invitation is simple - For 28 days I will provide you with 28 practical ways to generate more feelings of genuine happiness in your daily life.

So why 28 days if this isn't rehab?

28 days is what it takes to anchor a new habit.

'Cause being happy comes from making choices that become habits.

If happy habits weren't modeled for you by your family of origin - you probably aren't giving yourself the best chance at living your happiest life. So what you've got here is the step-by- step plan to anchor happiness habits in your waking world so you experience more natural highs and less lows. So if you are ready for more JOY, turn the page...

HOW THIS PROJECT BEGAN

A few years ago I watched the documentary, 'Happy' directed by Roko Belic. It's a beautiful film which journeys around the globe to meet some of the happiest people on Earth with the aim of sharing the specific lifestyle choices that account for their happy disposition. As well as being heart-warming and insightful, this film has enough awards to establish it as a 'must watch' piece of cinema history...(which I daresay created feelings of happiness in the director, despite the accolades posing some Feng Shui challenges.)

So I decided to watch the film again - this time to share it with my step-daughter who had just been accepted into film school, with the intent of inspiring her with the power she had to make a difference through the medium of film. As always, when you think you're being, 'Oh so benevolent!' suggesting what others need, it usually indicates the advice you personally need to follow. Such was the case in this instance.

I had just finished my busiest work year on record - 2014 'Year of the Horse'. A year that started with me deciding to birth more projects than a battery hen. So with that handicap I was not an odds on favorite in Year of the Horse. I started the year bolting out of the starting gates like I was riding high on a prize mare...a pace which could not be sustained over 365 days. I ended up finishing the year feeling like a novice jockey who'd been pulled behind the horse, trampled on by the rest of the pack and then retired early. Yes, it was time to review my work / life balance.

After watching the film I was brimming with inspiration and started making a list of all the things WE could do to create our happiest year yet! (Yes, I was roping my partner in.) I excitedly shared my list of FUN things to do with him, inviting him to join me in my mission to generate more JOY in our daily lives.

Then it occurred to me I could share the JOY with even more people via my community page on Facebook and create a happier world...(a devious ploy to keep me personally accountable). So I created an event on my community Facebook page, 'The Moon Woman' and within a week we had thousands of people around the world who also wanted to feel less stress and more of the good stuff.

We began on the lunar new year and each day people blew me away with their stories of how they had embraced the daily suggestion and reaped the benefits which they shared with those around them. People were still joining on the last day of the 28 day challenge and as we arrived at the end of our month together, no one wanted it to end. It was then people requested I put the info out as a book...so here it is!

It is my heart's intent that each page generates feelings of happiness in you.

Blessings, Tanishka

HOW TO USE THIS BOOK

AND GET THE MOST OUT OF IT

This is not a book you need to read from start to finish in order to grasp an overall concept. Instead, each new happiness habit is delivered in bite-sized chunks so you can process one new piece of info a day to integrate positive change, one step at a time.

You don't even have to read the 28 Happiness Habits in order. You may prefer to skim through the Table of Contents and start with the chapters that capture your attention.

To help you apply the ideas in your everyday life, every chapter ends with a 'call to action'. All change starts from within so reading insights every day will inspire us to take action, but it only through taking action that we really experience lasting positive change. So I encourage you to complete each chapter by doing the 'Call to Action'.

Finally, a study at the Dominican University of California found those who wrote down their goals, shared them and regularly reviewed them, maintained consistent accountability - making them 33% more likely to achieve their desired outcome.

So might I suggest 3 tips to ensure your happiest outcome...

Write down your goal in the form of a declaration to undertake 'The 28 Day Happiness Challenge' on your Facebook page. Alternatively, pin a note on your fridge, car dashboard, mirror or computer / phone screen saver.

Share the challenge and share the joy! Invite others to join you via your social media, email, group text or in person. If you work with a bunch of sad sacks this is a great strategy to improve team morale! Keep in mind it will be easier to do, the more people you invite. You may even want to ask people to sponsor you and donate the proceeds to the Art2Healing project. (Since all profits of the book go to the rehabilitation of sex traffic survivors and the prevention of girls being sold into a life of sex slavery I ask that you don't reproduce the daily Happiness

Habits but instead encourage your friends to buy a copy of the book as either an ebook or paperback to spread happiness amongst those who truly need it.)

You may like to set a reminder to review your life exactly a year after completing this challenge to examine the ways in which your life has been enriched, through applying the ideas presented. You may wish to do it as an annual community event or introduce it to different community groups as a community- building initiative. Invite people to check out www.28DayHappyChallenge.com for more info.

DAY 1: HAPPINESS HABIT

ALLOW EVERY COLOR OF EMOTION

Setting an intention is very powerful. Just by reading this book you are setting the intent to create a happier life. Like the old adage, 'Energy flows where attention goes' you will become aware of more opportunities to increase your happiness just by focusing your thoughts on ways to feel happy. That said, the way manifestation works is we often first attract the opposite to what we consciously ask to receive. We can throw a tanty about this and kick over the game-board and refuse to play anymore or we can consider why that is.

For every action there is also a reaction. So if we state to the benevolent universe, 'I want to be happy' we will then become more aware of the things in our life which do not make us happy. This is how the natural law of manifestation works; we set an intent and then confront our saboteur... this is kind of like the gatekeeper to our adventure!

So if we set an intent to be happy, our innate intelligence will start honing in on where, in our lives, we feel frustrated, depressed, angry or sad more than we feel content, fulfilled, enthusiastic or ecstatic.

This is an opportunity for us to examine the contributing factors to discern how we can have an impact on those factors, such as a shift in perspective or through being pro-active to address something.

MEETING THE SABOTEUR

So if you feel overwhelmed with how much your life sucks on day one of the Happy Challenge know you are not alone if you feel like throwing the towel in with a blanket statement like, 'Happy CHALLENGE is right! This isn't gonna work. I'm a moron for wasting my money on that dumb book' to justify abandoning your goal. Should you feel irritated by everything that just isn't going your way, take this as a sign that something has begun - something bigger than your rational self can comprehend is starting to shake things up. Yes, the benevolent universe is working with you in accordance with your intent to help you transform your life by shinning a flashlight into those dark corners where there is scant peace or soul fulfillment.

Allow me to demonstrate how this phenomenon played out for me the day before the Happy Challenge officially started...

I had a major attack of the SADS. I was pre-menstrual which certainly didn't help. (FYI - good to mark this time of the month on the calendar as whatever feelings have been suppressed during the month, will surface all at once! This is often overwhelming for women and our partners and kids.) So initially I was aware I felt heavy and apathetic about getting out of bed to start the day. I didn't want to get out of my bathrobe or leave the sanctuary of my bed. I felt very insular, like I could crawl into a ball and disappear just to have a break from feeling. There's the key word: Feeling!

(At forty-four I have felt these feelings many times, so I no longer fear them as a sign I will descend into depression for months. This is what I experienced in my younger years when I lacked the experiential wisdom and tools to process my own exploration of the shadowlands of my psyche.)

So I assessed the situation: 'I feel heavy because I am sitting on some unexpressed emotion'. In mysticism, the associated element of emotion is water. So if there's unexpressed emotion sitting below the surface needing to be released, we feel heavy energetically, physically and psychologically. (Just as you would lack a spring in your step if lugging full buckets of water!)

Despite my so-called awareness, I opted for DENIAL as my first point of defense. I think to myself, 'I'll cheer myself up by reading that book by a stand-up comic I was given for Christmas.' As a temporary measure this worked and I was able to escape my own thoughts and feelings by focusing on those of the author. So desperate was I too disassociate, I was so focused on the book I wasn't available to anyone else. Then - 'Coming, ready or not!' I was ambushed. I got to the last chapter and the author spoke about how much she loved her children and I was gone! Eclipsed by a torrent of grief. I felt a huge wave of deep sadness that my eleven year old daughter was living at the other end of the country (and in Australia that's not a day trip!) My feelings were in response to an external situation I felt powerless to change.

Choking back sobs, my rational self tried to step in to hold back the tidal wave of emotion by rationally reminding myself the current situation was ultimately a good thing, the balance we all needed after I had been her sole primary carer for eight and a half years. I also reassured myself it was the right decision because she was thriving, after having really reconnected with her Dad.

Whilst these thoughts did help me keep the situation in perspective, there was no escaping that my feelings still needed to be honored by being felt and expressed. Once I allowed myself to really feel the depth of what was in me and have 'a good cry' I felt cleansed, calmer and more centered in the acceptance of what was true and present, rather than the uneasy avoidance of it.

We all have situations in our lives that we feel powerless to change. Most of the time we may cope, but coping isn't the same thing as accepting. Since emotion is akin to the element of water, grief comes in waves. Some days the ocean is calm but other days we will experience a trigger, perhaps stormy conditions like pre-menstrual tension and we find ourselves in choppy seas. We have to learn to swim with the current and allow for the fact that we can't have blue skies every day.

So I'd like to encourage you to accept and express all your emotions - even if this means sometimes you will feel blue, grey or even black. We are a force of nature. Sometimes the forecast will be stormy with the possibility of flash-flooding, lightning strikes or hail. This is life when it is truly alive...feeling the extremes of all the elements. However, it is often through feeling our emotional intensity that we have our greatest flashes of insight and find our greatest strength, which catalyzes great personal understanding and power.

So just like a woman giving birth, if you are contracting in fear - not wanting to feel the pain of your current situation - BRING IT ON! The more you resist

feeling, the longer and more drawn out the process will be. So risk feeling out of your mind with grief, fear or rage temporarily or you will need to numb yourself with substances or distractions and merely exist rather than feel truly alive.

If you want to experience great joy, then you must accept that also means being willing to feel great sorrow. So if you're ready for a rebirth, enter into your fears and emotions. If you're used to disassociating or numbing, use a catalyst to reconnect with your feelings, such as a movie, song or old photos. Dare to feel! For it is through our ability to feel, that we stir up and release the blocked energy which has kept us from feeling fully alive! Once we dare to feel the uncomfortable feelings we swing to the other polarity and we experience the opposite. So the more sadness we release, the lighter and happier we feel. Whereas the more sadness we hang on to, for fear of it overwhelming us, the longer we stay stuck in sadness and can't move on.

We instinctually know this as babies. This is why babies appear so Zen, crying uncontrollably and then ten minutes later belly laughing just as freely. They don't judge their emotions, they just feel them and move on. We only learn to suppress our emotions to the degree those around us aren't comfortable with emotion being expressed. We then mimic the ways they swallow their unexpressed emotion with painkillers, alcohol, cheesecake or pot, just as babies are given a pacifier rather than held and encouraged to let out their feelings.

So rather than bag our parents for not being perfect, we need to allow ourselves the freedom to express the full spectrum of human emotion. It is our feelings make us truly human and to deny our humanity is a one way ticket to living in a state of torment. So, contrary to crude expectations, this challenge does not infer we walk away with smiles perpetually pasted to our faces like 'Botox' clones of 'Ken and Barbie'. Rather, we honor our full range of feeling, knowing it is the pathway to human happiness.

CALL TO ACTION

Most of us have been conditioned to feel uncomfortable with openly expressing our vulnerability. To reframe the perception that vulnerability equals weakness, watch this great clip from Brene Brown and find out why the happiest people in the world are the ones who truly dare to express their deep, dark and uncomfortable feelings.

http://www.ted.com/talks/brene_brown_on_vulnerability

DAY 2: HAPPINESS HABIT

ATTUNE TO THE MOON

Just as you wouldn't go out in the middle of Winter wearing light cotton shorts and a singlet, it makes just as much sense to consider the effect of the lunar weather on our moods and emotions. This is not lunacy, in fact the opposite - to avoid feeling looney we need only live in tune with lunar cycle as a way to create greater emotional balance.

If you don't think the moon has any effect on your moods, consider the effect the moon has on the tides of every ocean the world over. Since we are comprised of over 70% water, it stands to reason that the moon also has a huge impact on the rise and fall of our inner emotional tides.

This is why statistics show higher admissions to crises facilities like hospital E.R's and police stations during the full moon lunar phase each month. Crises occur when our emotions run high. More so, for those people who are already living life on the edge, as they feel less able to contain their emotional overwhelm, which then spills over, affecting the emotional wellbeing of those nearest to them. So how do we avoid going feral like a werewolf at full moon and ripping up daises in our neighbor's yard?

Understand the moon phases and the effect they have on our psyche.

NAVIGATING THE LUNAR PHASES

There are four main phases. The more we schedule our plans to match the rise and fall of our personal energy levels in accordance with these phases, the less chance we have of having a meltdown. This is especially important info for women to take note of, since the moon also affects our hormonal cycle - even if our physical monthly cycle has ceased. This is why women are more emotionally sensitive. (On the upside, once we understand our emotional cycle and learn to steer our ship, we can harness our psychic and emotional sensitivity as a gift rather than fearing our emotional self as 'the mad diva' who can strike without warning.) Note: Men who have a lot of planets in Cancer in their natal chart or planets in the fourth house (which is ruled by Cancer) will also be more prone to moon-induced mood swings. This is because Cancer is ruled by the moon.

NEW MOON: This is akin to low tide and occurs two weeks after full moon. During this phase we are more likely to feel tired and grumpy. This low ebb of lunar energy can cause us to feel emotionally down, passive, depressed, inward and powerless. It is when we are more likely to see ourselves as the victim in situations. This is a danger time for those prone to self-harm, comfort eating, addictions or suicidal fantasies.

HOW TO BALANCE YOUR EMOTIONS AT NEW MOON:

Get enough sleep, eat nutritious food (freeze extra food in the lead up to new moon so you don't have to cook), avoid sad films, music and people who drain you. Meditate, have baths, journal and spend time with people who nurture you and support you to see the blessing and strengths you have in your current situation. (This is why indigenous women gathered in Red Tents and Moon Lodges at new moon. To find out more about how to reclaim this ancient tradition at New Moon see the Resources section.)

FIRST QUARTER MOON: We can feel adventurous, independent, social and playful. This is an ideal time to catch up with friends, go on a date, step out of your comfort zone by going somewhere new, trying something you haven't done before or taking a leap of faith on your skills and talents.

FULL MOON: This phase occurs two weeks after new moon and is the opposite extreme. Full moon is when we can feel manic, aggressive, impatient, scattered and impulsive. This is a danger time for those with a tendency to be over-doers or workaholics, as they tend to snap and make mistakes as the emotional intensity builds.

HOW TO BALANCE YOUR EMOTIONS AT FULL MOON:

Try to unplug from screens one hour before bed and give yourself a settling routine such as reading or a hot bath or shower before bed. As your body temp cools you'll find it easier to relax into sleep, otherwise you will experience insomnia, especially if you're not in bed before 10pm when the lunar energy rises to a peak at midnight and doesn't wane until 2am. If you are overtired, your fuse will be shorter the following day. Avoid caffeine in the afternoon and evening. If the full moon falls on a night where you don't have to work the next day and you don't have young kids, enjoy the party time of full moon and stay up dancing, knowing you can sleep in.

LAST QUARTER MOON: We can feel like canceling plans and staying in as we slow down and re-group, processing the month that was. This is an ideal time to journal, plan quiet play activities with our kids, do gentle exercise, such as walks in nature and decrease the amount of external stimulus, so we have the space to hear ourselves think.

CALL TO ACTION

To experience more emotional grace and harmony in your life, try the following...

STEP ONE: Look up the new and full moon dates for the year. You can Google them or get my Moon Woman phone app which has this info, along with daily advice on how to flow with the moon sign and phase each day. (see Resources.)

STEP TWO: Mark these two extreme moon phase days in your diary / calendar for each month so you can take into account the energies and plan accordingly. You can also buy moon diaries / calendars which indicate the lunar phases and transits.

This awareness will help you to not make demands of yourself and others when they're at their lowest ebb or most stressed, which can then result in conflict.

DAY 3: HAPPINESS HABIT

INCREASE YOUR GOOD VIBRATIONS

Do you find yourself regularly singing jingles from TV and radio ads that pop into your head? If you are exposed to commercial radio or television, it's pretty much inevitable since they are designed to be catchy and memorable. Repetition is how we learn. So repeating an ad slogan (even in the privacy of our own mind) anchors that message within our psyche. Since the primary aim of corporations is to motivate us to consume, this is not a wise practice for those seeking inner happiness free of corporate dependence.

As with any habit, we can't simply 'give it up' without having another habit to replace it with. So to assist with that, might I suggest reclaiming your inner jukebox from corporations telling you what to think, say and do with some new lyrics and melodies penned by those who most resonate with your soul's truth. Yes! It's time to gift yourself some new 'feel good' music!

Whether you listen to commercial radio / TV or not, treating yourself to some new 'choons' is guaranteed to lift your spirits.

Why? Music is the fastest way to change our vibrational state. Since all matter is made up of oscillating particles of energy, when we listen to 'good vibrations' it calms our energy field, kind of like a sonic massage. This soothes our nervous system, reducing our stress levels. When we consider stress is the underlying cause of most relationship conflict and ill health, it certainly pays to invest in some good music on a regular basis. (It is also nicer than spending your cash on medicine or mediation!)

BE DISCERNING WITH YOUR CHOICE OF MUSIC

In the early 1970's, Dorothy Retallack performed a series of experiments on plants involving various forms of music. The plants that were played soothing music grew to a uniform size with lush, green foliage. Whereas the plants exposed to rock music wilted and died. Out of all the music played, classical Indian music produced the best results and the plants were completely indifferent to country and western music.

Similarly, in the 1990's Masaru Emoto did experiments on the effect that different energies had on the structure of water molecules. Despite a backlash of scientists attacking him for not conducting his experiments under the controlled conditions in- keeping with scientific convention, his book, showing the photos of his evidence became a New York Times bestseller. Again, classical and soothing music produced harmonious outcomes, with intricate mandalas forming in the water molecules which contrasted with the dissonant fractured shapes created in response to rock music. To see the results for yourself visit:

http://www.unitedearth.com.au/watercrystals.html

Since we are also organic beings, made up of the elements we can also use music to enhance feelings of emotional wellbeing based on our perception of reality.

In 2009 Nidhya Logeswaran and Joydeep Bhattacharya from the University of London, did an experiment to determine how exposure to various styles of music affects how we perceive visual images. In their experiment, thirty subjects were presented with a series of happy or sad excerpts of music. They were then shown a photograph of a face. Whatever the expression, they perceived it to be more happy or sad depending on the piece of music they had just heard. This illustrates how receiving sound through our aural sense effects how we also see the world!

I can personally attest to the power of music upon my physical health. As a child I had chronic illness up until the age of twelve. From the age of twelve I started singing lessons and every morning would do an hour of singing practice before going to school. In order for my singing teacher to take me on as a pupil, I also had to agree to join the local choral society, comprised of about fifty senior citizens. From then on, I was well.

Years later I became aware of the kundalini yogic practice of Chakra Toning. This involves singing the Sanskrit tone for each energy center in order of the ascending and descending notes of the scale. The changing frequency of sound opens, clears and strengthens the vortices of energy in our personal matrix, promoting health, vitality and well being. I have recorded this practice on CD and as an MP3 for others wanting to sing their morning meditation! (See Resources.)

If Sanskrit toning isn't your bag - take lessons to learn an instrument that's always appealed to you or have a regular jam night with friends using anything you can find to produce a sound - including your voices to scat and chant. Or if you have a friend who can play guitar, invite them over for a sing-a-long around a fire. If disco is more your scene, go to a karaoke bar, rent a karaoke machine or buy a Singstar game on Wii or XBox and belt out your favorite tunes. Alternatively, a lot of community centers now have regular drumming circles with spare drums for newcomers.

CALL TO ACTION

JOIN A COMMUNITY CHOIR: My partner, Michael has been in a community choir for fourteen years. They have seen each other through births, deaths and everything in between. Regardless of what's happening in their lives, they come together and sing heart- warming songs, from a repertoire of world music, folk, pop and gospel. There is something deeply healing about a community coming together to let their voices out with the intent of creating harmony. It affirms we can all get along, regardless of age, gender, culture or social standing. To view the healing power of a community choir watch 'As It Is In Heaven' nominated for an Academy Award for best foreign film in 2005.

GET SOME NEW MUSIC: If that ol' saboteur has raised it's head with, 'I can't afford new music' consider these resourceful ways to get some...

Go to your local library and borrow some CD's

Swap some music with a friend

Listen to one of the many internet radio stations

Listen to some of your favorite artists on You Tube

CREATE A HAPPY PLAYLIST: Like the old mixed tape, but digital - put together a list of MP3's you can listen to in the car during rush hour or whilst navigating after school traffic or driving your kids to various activities to make it always a pleasure. Here's some of my happy music suggestions...hope they make you feel good.

Happy by Pharrell Williams

Joy to the World by Three Dog Night

A Beautiful Day by India Arie

Signed, Sealed, Delivered by Stevie Wonder

We'll Be Together by Sting

Corner of the Earth by Jamiroqui Here Comes the Sun by The Beatles *Feeling*

Good by Nina Simone

I'm Yours by Jason Miraz

and The Greatest Hits of Al Green!

DAY 4: HAPPINESS HABIT

SPEND QUALITY TIME WITH YOUR SOUL CLAN

Spend time with people you love. Seems obvious, but knowing and doing are two different things and often weeks, months - even years can go by and we wonder how long it's been since we saw people who we really adore.

When we connect with people who truly see and understand us, our energy field brightens and strengthens as their presence affirms our light. Whereas when we spend time with those who don't have a shared value system or interests, we retract our energy and feel small.

Unfortunately, due to balancing the responsibilities of modern life, we can spend more time interacting with people due to circumstance, rather than by conscious choice. This occurs when we attend work or family functions out of a sense of duty rather than prioritize seeing the people who really raise our spirits. This is not uncommon. In fact, since the industrial revolution, it has become commonplace for people to spend more time with their work colleagues than their partners or children.

This makes it even more important for us to make it a priority to spend quality time with our favorite people. (Not just sharing or discussing what chores have to be done.) Trust that your mind will always find a reason it would be more logical to get something done, such as yard work, housework or schoolwork, so we have to make a conscious effort to also allow the heart to make some more of our decisions and do something which doesn't always sound sensible but will leave us feeling on a high!

NOT SOMETHING ELSE I HAVE TO ORGANIZE!

When we feel overwhelmed with the list of responsibilities tugging on us, the thought of entertaining can fill us with instant dread and exhaustion. So we need to find efficient ways to get our quality social and intimate fixes. The key is to ensure our ongoing human need for friendship isn't reduced to a one-off event. This is done by making a monthly or weekly date. Then you don't have to re-invest time organizing schedules to ensure it happens again. Simply take your diary or pocket organizer with you and set a reminder to meet up again once a month to avoid time passing without any contact.

For even one hour spent with someone you can really share a good belly laugh with will lighten your week's stresses and recharge you so you approach everything on your plate with good humor. This is especially important for us as we get older. For, as young singles, we often live close to our friends and see them often but as many of us marry and then move to the suburbs in order to raise children or relocate to pursue our careers, it can seem all too hard to make the effort to catch up with our friends on a regular basis.

We need social variety, not just intimacy if we are to stay open, receptive to new ideas and in touch with the world around us. If we are feeling low or perceive we aren't doing as well in life as we think we could be, there can be a tendency to hide away rather than risk being seen in our vulnerability. However, the more insular we become, the harder it is for us to move beyond our own imposed limitations. So do look for and embrace opportunities to socialize with people of all ages and from all walks of life, by connecting with community initiatives and spending time doing the things you love, to find people on your wavelength. Otherwise our world can narrow down to the people we share our domestic and working life with, leaving us feeling socially alienated and intimidated to form meaningful social connections that would really enrich our lives.

Spending time socializing independently from your partner or family also enlivens those relationships by stimulating us with fresh experiences and perspectives to share with our significant others. It also helps to remind us that we are more than the roles we play in our day-to-day interactions of partner, parent, boss or employee and takes the pressure off unconsciously expecting our partner to fulfill all our needs, which can lead to petty resentments.

So take a moment to consider if there are any activities that you used to love doing on a regular basis but stopped doing because the people in your current life circumstances aren't into them. Then consider who in your social network might enjoy catching up to do that with you on a regular basis. Alternatively many cities and towns now have 'meet-up' groups who gather in a public place to share a common interest.

Similarly, you may have stopped spending time with someone because your partner doesn't enjoy their company. Instead of pruning that limb completely to accommodate your spouse, make a date to catch up with your estranged friend away from the home front so your partner is spared, while you rekindle your friendship.

In my work as a couples coach I saw many men lose touch with their friends once they married and had kids, as they left all the social arrangements to their wives. This meant their entire social life revolved around their wives social network, which created a social dependency and subsequent disempowerment. It takes a bit of effort to maintain friendships, something which women tend to value and invest more time in than men, who are often more solitary creatures. Older men in particular can feel socially awkward calling up a friend to invite them to do something, so creating a reason can be helpful if it has been a while since your last contact, such as asking their advice or needing their assistance with a task that is a two-man job. In Australia we have an organization called, 'The Men's Shed' which is a meeting place for men of all ages to share various crafts as a   focal   point   for   social   interaction.   Here's   the   link: http://www.mensshed.org/home/.aspx

Online social networks also make it really easy to catch up with people from our past, so if there's someone who you've lost contact with but would love to reconnect with, dare to do a search and send them a message. Thanks to technology, distance is no longer an excuse to not spend regular time with friends living interstate or abroad. With free video calls on downloadable apps like Skype we can have intimate face-to-face chats for hours and never spend a Friday night eating dinner alone! This may also include catching up with your siblings, cousins or grandparents!

CALL TO ACTION

Today I invite you to reconnect with someone whose company you truly enjoy. This may be a dear friend or a favorite relative.

STEP ONE: Write a list of all your favorite people. (If you've become insular you may need to look through your address book or contacts list to jog your memory). You could throw a party to reconnect with many people at once, but I've found you never get to spend any quality time with anyone at a large gathering. So if it's been a while, start off with a one-on-one meeting or smaller gathering.

STEP TWO: Suggest regular dates to catch up on a cyclic basis, such as at the same time each month and write the dates in both your calendars. (Since a month is an emotional cycle, this will help keep your emotions high having monthly contact.)

STEP THREE: Consider making it the same place and the same time so you don't have to spend time organizing details every month. The easier it is to maintain, the more likely you will follow through regularly. For example, have breakfast at the same cafe, Skype at the same time and day that fits with both schedules and time zones or have coffee and cake the first Sunday of every month.

When we invest time in that which truly nurtures us we feel supported, joyful and relaxed. These qualities then permeate the other areas of our lives - decreasing stress and enhancing the quality of all our other interactions.

DAY 5: HAPPINESS HABIT

BLESS INSTEAD OF CURSE

I recall a wonderful speech my dear friend, Nick made for his fiftieth birthday. Nick is a composer and sound healer and he spoke about how he had become aware that he no longer wished to swear. Not from a moral standpoint but from a vibrational perspective. Now let it be known I have always enjoyed having a colorful vocabulary of expletives, but the point he raised led me to reflect upon my study of voice production and phonetics as a teenager. Swear words are most often formed with plosive consonants - they being: p, b, c, f, d, t and k. For these sounds allow us to express energy in a way that is explosive, relieving the pent up energy we need to express.

When we have a negative intention behind these sounds they are as volatile as hot oil spitting from a frying pan, especially when directed towards someone. This is because 'cuss' words are dissonant in their intent, so they clash and fragment the energy field between us and others, heightening the vibration of anger by creating a miasma of emotional energy known as a 'thought form'. When we live in a home where we swear a lot, this vibration gathers within the four walls, creating an air of struggle rather than grace.

So too, when we make a habit of swearing we create a 'thought form' energetically around ourselves. When we understand the universal law of attraction, that being that 'like attracts like' we can see how walking around in a sound cloud which affirms a reality of frustration and anger is going to attract people and events which vibrate at a similar rate of shadow density.

HOW TO MINIMIZE SWEARING

I don't recommend trying to quit swearing 'cold turkey'...or you'll feel inauthentic - like you woke up possessed by Ned Flanders. (The do-gooder from the TV show, 'The Simpsons'.) Sure you may start out, pleased with how well-behaved you are, then end up suppressing so much frustration and unexpressed expletives that they end up coming out at the one time at the worst possible moment, such as your aunt's funeral or 5 year old's birthday party.

As stated earlier...with any habit, unless we focus on replacing the old behavior with a more positive one we won't be able to give it away. (Personally I don't recommend a swear jar, as this creates a dynamic whereby your children feel entitled to police your behavior and issue infringement notices which makes your self- worth smaller than the amount of coins in the jar.)

Instead, consider why you swear. Since we don't do anything without getting a pay-off, there are ways in which swearing serves you or you wouldn't do it. Do you swear to fit in with your cultural peers? Are you acting tough in an effort to 'keep it all together' so you don't risk acknowledging how vulnerable you feel? Are you doing it to rebel against your parents...even if you moved out twenty years ago? Do you get a kick out of shock value? Do you just have so much anger inside of you that's it's got to come out your mouth to avoid creating bowel cancer?

So make a list of all the pay-off's you personally get from swearing.

Now consider other ways you can address those needs. Do you need to seek out people you can socialize with whom you don't need to project an image of bravado? (This can be true of both men and women, particularly if working in male-dominated professions.) Do you need to seek out more emotional support, such as a sharing circle or counseling session so you have a space to express your vulnerability on a regular basis in a safe space? Do you need to forgive your parents? Perhaps you need to find other ways to express your individuality or get hypnotherapy to address your inner rage.

Once you've addressed getting your needs met in healthier ways, you can entertain alternative words to use in moments of frustration.

You could have fun with it and try and come up with as many nonsensical words which start with plosive consonants to use when pushed beyond your coping abilities - however, the words must feel fulfilling in the moment or you will experience a loss of personal power if you feel inauthentic. (Please note: if you hit your thumb with a hammer or get stung by a wasp by all means let rip with every sound known to man without any thought of self-judgement.)

Breathe easy, fellow swearers...I'm not suggesting we banish swear words completely from our modern-day vernacular. What I am suggesting, as mere food for thought, is that since it has become more publicly acceptable to swear, many of us have become lazy with our choice of language and so we will swear as our default setting, rather than find a more creative option to express ourselves. So perhaps start a habit of consulting your dictionary or thesaurus to expand your vocabulary.

Another practice I have adopted in the past few years which feels good and helps spread the good stuff is the habit of blessing, rather than cursing. Yep, whatever happens - I try to ensure my first response is to say, 'blessings' or 'bless them'. Blessing helps shift the energy from a negative into a positive. It also allows the space for a negative to transform into a positive. Whereas if we judge a situation as bad, we may limit the chance of a positive outcome. When we acknowledges that whilst something may appear at first to be a curse, it may turn out to be a blessing...we affirm our trust in the infinite intelligence of the Universe. (I offer a parable which illustrates this on Day 25's Happiness Habit: Focus on the Positive.)

Einstein said the most powerful question we can ask is, 'Is it a benevolent Universe?' For if we believe it to be so, that will be our subjective experience. So too, when we bless all that happens, we feel blessed and that becomes our experience of reality. That shift in perspective then helps us to see the blessing in every situation, rather than focusing on the negative. If we consider swearing in this light, we can see it does the opposite, it affirms life is a struggle.

If we also understand that whatever energy or intent we send out returns to us magnified, you can see how our life becomes truly blessed with serendipity when we create a habit of blessing everything that happens. This practice helps raise our personal vibration, along with the vibration of any situation or event,

so the highest possible outcome can manifest. As a result, blessing feels good. So much so, it's addictive. At the risk of sounding like a nun

once you start, you can't stop!

For those worried about what others will think. Know this! I have never had someone respond negatively to being blessed. It is like a smile - it's a free gift that says we wish the highest good for the other person. So regardless of their belief system, they receive our good intention for them. In fact I have seen it take people off- guard and melt their hard exterior. Most of all blessing is a small but powerful act we can do to create a more loving world. It says I am not afraid to encounter all in my path with an open heart in perfect love and perfect trust.

CALL TO ACTION

Try it for one day...bless everything that happens and see how it feels. Here are some examples...

–   When I pay people, I say, 'Blessings' in gratitude for their product or service - this infuses the payment with the energy of love which will passed on to many.

–   When people pay me, I say, 'Blessings and may it return to you three-fold' in gratitude for their trust in me and to affirm their ongoing abundance.

–   When I speak of someone I say, 'Bless them'.

–   When I exclaim in response to a situation, which could be judged good or bad, I say 'Bless' which energetically helps restore harmony through intent.

–   I bless all my meals and all those involved in the food chain.

–   I bless beverages when I make them, by placing my hand over them and sending loving intent from the energy center in the palm of my hand.

DAY 6: HAPPINESS HABIT

KEEP YOUR CUP OF SELF-LOVE FULL

As stated in the previous chapter, we live in a holographic universe. This is a realization known by mystics down through the ages which was later qualified by physicist, David Bohm, a respected colleague and friend of Albert Einstein. It simply means whatever we perceive to be a universal truth will indeed become our reality.

So if we project that 'Everybody hates me, nobody loves me...think I'll go and eat worms.' That will prove to be true. It also illustrates how physics ensures we learn the lesson of the idiom, 'Treat others the way you want to treated' since others will mirror our behavior back to us. Similarly, we must treat ourselves with loving kindness or others will mirror the miserly and neglectful attitude we perpetuate on ourselves.

For if we aren't aware of our needs, give to ourselves last or negate our needs by repeating mantras that affirm our lack, such as, 'You can't afford that' we demonstrate to others how to treat us and we end up being taken for granted. In addition, when we do give to others, we often do so from a place of duty, since we're anchoring the victim / martyr pendulum with our self-sacrificing behaviors.

This is when, understandably, giving becomes tinged with feelings of resentment and an unspoken need to be given something in return - such as spending more time with us or giving them a degree of authority over our lives, either of which burdens the receiver with a sense of obligation or manipulation. This is especially important to acknowledge, when we consider most of our communication is non-verbal. So it is inevitable that others pick up on our unspoken thoughts and feelings and this influences how they feel toward us. True giving is only when something is given freely, with no strings attached - when no conditions apply. Otherwise it is not an act of giving, but an act of control, be it overt or covert.

ALTRUIST VS NARCISSIST

Often those who want to prove to themselves they are a 'good person' strive to be seen as an altruist - an 'all-giving' provider / nurturer due to a fear of being selfish or perceived as self-centered. This is not a sustainable ideal to try and uphold. For unless we identify our needs in a situation and speak up on our own behalf to meet them, we end up so burnt-out or sick, we end up becoming a burden to those around us. So it is in everyone's interests that we exercise self-care and educate those around us that everyone's needs are equal and need to be honored as such. This attitude is rife in care professions, such as holistic wellbeing, childcare, healthcare, aged and disability care - not just amongst the service providers themselves, but in the general public's perception that those working in these areas should give without asking for anything or very little in return. These professions are all feminine polarity vocations, indicating how we can all contribute to shifting the status of the feminine in our society.

CALL TO ACTION

STEP ONE: IDENTIFY AND COMMUNICATE YOUR NEEDS.

Take a moment to consider to whom you sense any feelings of resentment. Then consider what needs you feel you have, which are not being met. This is especially important if you have been hearing yourself sigh with a heavy heart or noticed yourself feeling envious of others. Or if you've harbored feelings of being unappreciated. Now consider how you can let those involved know specifically what your needs, are so they can help you shoulder the load, minimizing your frustration and potential martyrdom.

STEP TWO: ATTUNE TO YOUR HEART.

Next, close your eyes and take your awareness into your heart and ask, 'What are my heart's deepest desires?' Your response may come in the form of ideas, images, feelings or impressions. There's no one way or right way to receive your heart's knowing.

STEP THREE: FILL YOUR OWN CUP.

Before we can be loving towards others, we must first be generous toward ourselves. For when our cup of self-love is full, we naturally express the overflow outwards to others. So instead of waiting for someone to 'make you happy' or rescue you from your unhappiness - make the commitment to be loyal to your own needs by actively being your own best friend. This following activity will help you fill your cup to overflowing! Love is a verb...a doing word. It involves taking action and charity begins at home.

– Draw a large goblet that fills a page on a sheet of paper.

– Write down all the things that you enjoy and can give to yourself. Please Note: This is not a bucket list to get around to before you die but a list you start doing today! For example: brunches with friends, fresh flowers in the house, new music, face masques, candlelit bubble baths, clothes swaps with friends, coloring mandalas, baking, reading a good book, picnics, walks in nature, board-game nights, massages and Kirtan chanting.

– Do one thing a week and cross it off the list as you go. Each thing you do will fill up your cup of self-love. This needs to become a habit so your cup doesn't become so empty that you have nothing left to give. Let this be a springboard for being generous towards yourself - from throwing away your desperation undies (the ones where the elastic has seen better days, even though they were once faves) to ensuring you give yourself those small, 'Ahhhh' moments regularly like getting into clean sheets or slipping into a warm bath.

DAY 7: HAPPINESS HABIT

ACKNOWLEDGE AND CELEBRATE YOUR

MILESTONES!

Life offers us a series of challenges which help us to grow. Each challenge teaches us something about ourselves so our character can develop. So if we don't take the time to acknowledge what we've achieved, learned or transcended through the marking of time, we can feel as if life is just a constant struggle with no real purpose.

In our youth worshiping culture, many middle-age and elderly people stop celebrating their birthday. This is because they view the natural process of aging negatively, so they don't want to focus on it or draw attention to it. When we stop acknowledging a milestone, we rob ourselves of the opportunity to process what that achievement or transition means to us - an awareness which reconnects us with how we feel about ourselves. Without this introspection, we often fail to take the steps needed to address the issues that accompany each life change.

In particular, many people fear milestone birthdays such as their fortieth, fiftieth or sixtieth, for fear they won't live up to their ego's expectations - such as what they think they should've achieved, how their life should look like or expectations they should look eternally young.

Confronting how we feel about ourselves and our life on a regular basis is healthy. Milestones assist us to do this. They mark the passage of time which invites us to review how our values and priorities have changed. Without this cyclic period of self- reflection we end up judging ourselves by standards that don't reflect our current life stage.

Acknowledging our milestones along the winding road that forms our unique life journey also gives us the opportunity to process each chapter and make our peace with it so we are better able to embrace our current situation. It also helps us to check-in and identify whether we need additional support, to assist us in transitioning from one phase to the next, so we can mature with grace and step forward confidently with no regrets.

As an intuitive reader for twenty years most of the work I did was assisting people to acknowledge changes that needed to be made in their lives, giving them various tools to assist them with their transition. This led to me creating and facilitating rite of passage ceremonies, an ancient practice common to all indigenous cultures. These ancient civilizations recognized the importance of mentoring for each life transition, along with a sacred ceremony to help one acknowledge the psychological death and rebirth needed during every major life transition. Without this wisdom and support, people fear change and aging which creates anxiety, self-judgement and depression.

We have many milestones throughout our lives, including:

- birthdays
- finishing primary / elementary / high school
- puberty
- first job
- leaving home
- first love / break-up / loss of virginity
- college / university graduation
- engagement / wedding
- bachelor / bachelorette parties
- pregnancy / birth
- loss of a loved one (including pets)
- business / project / creative endeavor launch
- children's birthdays
- separation / divorce
- anniversaries
- menopause
- job loss
- illness / depression
- relocation

If we lack the support needed during one of our major milestones, we find the subsequent special days a huge challenge. For example, after the death of a parent, Mother's Day will be a testing time or after a relationship ends, our first Valentine's Day may evoke another wave of grief.

Each season and holiday are also milestones which carry a heightened charge, depending on the memories we associate with them. as they give us an opportunity to stop, reflect on the passing of time and share what we've done or learned.

CALL TO ACTION

Today you're going to consider how you can celebrate your times of transition, rather than fearing or overlooking them. This will affirm life is worth living and who you are and what you have done is worth celebrating.

So consider your most recent milestone by journaling how you feel about it. This will illuminate if there are any unresolved issues you could use some mentoring on. (Look at the list above for suggestions.)

Now consider to read next contemplate how you could mark a milestone in your life or in the life of someone special to you, in one of the following ways:

- Hold a theme or surprise party
- Hire a celebrant to create a rite of passage ceremony
- Create a slideshow of images of that chapter
- Make a seasonal altar with found objects of beauty
- Decorate their desk with balloons or car with a 'Just Married' sign
- Light candles
- Design a scrap book
- Toast with champagne
- Go out for dinner
- Have professional photos done
- Plan a launch to birth an event, project or business
- Go away for the weekend

Life is what we make it. So the more we embrace and celebrate the journey - all of it - the more rich and meaningful our lives feel. Don't be afraid to share your milestones with those around you, as it is an honor to witness a pivotal moment in someone's life.

These memories are what we will recall as our highlights when we look back on our life. Definitely something making time for.

'Do not regret growing older, it is a privilege denied to many.'
Author Unknown.

DAY 8: HAPPINESS HABIT

COMMUNE WITH MOTHER NATURE

For those of you who have watched the film, 'Happy' which inspired this book, you may recall the man who felt like the luckiest man alive because he spent time every day in awe at the natural beauty of the Bayou. (If you haven't seen the film check out the link in the Resources section.) Time spent alone communing with Mother Nature helps us to slow down our endless thoughts and come home to our hearts. Our hearts are the core of who we are and the center of our being, so his shift in our awareness enables us to see the world through our soul, instead of our analytical mind, which in turn helps us to be more accepting and patient with ourselves and those around us.

Nature encourages us to be natural and relax the facade we may try to project in social situations, so we can be true to who we really are inside. This helps us to be authentic and not care so much about what others think. One needs only look at how much people in the city worry more about how they are perceived compared to those who live in the country to realize the degree to which this is true.

Spending time with Mother Nature also helps put our human struggles in perspective, reducing our stress levels. Whereas, when we disconnect from nature, we tend to stress over isolated incidents, which inevitably occur, that we can't control. The degree to which we lose touch with the source of life itself, that being nature, indicates the degree to which we respond from a place of fear or acceptance. When our locus of reality is upon the unnatural world, such as the man-made construct of time, our stress levels multiply as we convince ourselves that everything hinges on the one event in our life that we are facing, rather than keeping in mind that it is what we learn from the sum of our life experiences that is most important. When we reconnect with the natural world we are reminded that life will go on, regardless of the outcome of our latest challenge. This is humbling for our rational mind, who can get so caught up in the details, that we lose sight of the big picture.

The longer our disconnection from nature, the more we forget just how good spending time in nature makes us feel. This is because nature recharges us with negative ions in the oxygen we breathe, which helps us relax from a highly charged positive or active state. Having direct contact with the elements of creation, such as air, soil, water and fire also help us to recharge. It is interesting to note that the vibrational frequency of Mother Earth matches our own heartbeat, so attuning our heart to the Mother is as simple as taking a walk in nature.

In Japan, the practice of 'Shinrin-yoku' (forest bathing) has inspired forty-eight forest therapy trails due to research showing time spent communing in a forest decreases stress-related disorders including anxiety, depression and anger and diseases like diabetes and cancer. Source: Kendra Pieree-Lewis, author of 'Green Washed: Why We Can't Buy Our Way To A Green Planet'. She goes on to say in the USA there was a fifty percent decline in the amount of time children spent outside between 1997 and 2003. Nowadays the average US citizen spends ninety percent of their time indoors, due to the amount of time we spend online, on social media, watching movies or gaming in virtual words. Yet, when we do spend time at the beach, camping and walking in the fresh air of the wilderness, we wonder why we don't do it more often.

The reason we often make time in nature low on our list of priorities is due to our productivity focused mind not seeing the value of spending quiet time with nature. It's often not until we're completely at our wit's end that we concede we need some time out to recuperate. The mind, despite its best intentions will often anchor 'stress habits' in its effort to get everything done. This leads us to become tightly wound, chasing the never-ending demands of the mind that we fail to see how we're becoming more insular and less available to ourselves and those around us. It is this habitual state of stress, prolonged isolation and separation which causes a fertile foundation for dis-ease within our subtle bodies, which if not addressed, eventually manifests as physical symptoms to alert us to our unhealthy way of living.

The more time we spend resting in the gentle, non-judgmental and revitalizing energy of nature, the more we create a state conducive to growth and happiness. I often get my best ideas walking in the forest when I'm not even focusing on solving anything, just communing with my surrounds. For it is this state of oneness which connects us to the collective consciousness and universal intelligence. This is not new information. In fact, I daresay there is not one among you who doesn't already know this. The power lies, not in the knowing, but in the doing.

CALL TO ACTION

Make a commitment to gift yourself even one moment today to reconnect with Mother Nature...and continue this once a day. Even if you live in the city, consider setting a reminder to interact with the elements of life to renew your Spirit. Taste the snow, dance in the rain, gaze at the moon, walk to work through the park, read the shapes of clouds, stare into a log fire, talk to a ladybird, write a poem about a flower, run through crunchy dry leaves or hug a tree.

I recommend dawn or dusk, as these are the high times when the veils between the worlds are thinnest, making communion with all the realms most magical. This is also the most beautiful time of day as the colors of sunrise and sunset bestow a golden light upon everything. This is the time of Sacred Union every day, when the animal kingdom sing songs of praise for the gift of life. Be part of this daily miracle in exaltation with existence and your heart will be filled anew every day.

DAY 9: HAPPINESS HABIT

NURTURE YOURSELF WITH WHOLESOME FOOD

In my early twenties I went to see a traditional Chinese doctor who's I'd been told did massage on the medical health scheme. I confided in him I was experiencing depression and he responded by asking me about my diet. He explained there was no point examining my mental or emotional health if we didn't start with the state of my physical health, since that was the foundation upon which our emotional and mental state rests. This approach makes sense when we consider the structure of our energetic body.

If we explore a little deeper we also incorporate an awareness of our energetic body. Within our energy body we have seven major energy centers which are located along the central nervous cord within our spines. These energy centers underpin the state of our physical, emotional and mental health. In Sanskrit these vortices are called chakras. When they become blocked we experience imbalance and disease in the organs and subtle bodies they govern. Where as when they are clear, we experience vitality and good health. This is why the ancient symbol of the caduceus is the symbol for good medicine.

The bottom chakra governs our physical health, the second chakra governs our emotional health and the third chakra, our mental health. So it stands to reason that if we hope to feel emotionally and mentally balanced, we need to first ensure our physical health is attended to, which then supports our emotional and mental wellbeing.

CALL TO ACTION

LISTEN TO YOUR BODY.

I'm not a nutritionist but in the twenty-odd years since that visit, I've learned to listen more to my body and identify what made a positive impact on my health and what didn't. The older I get, the more I am humbled by how important our health is, so as a result, my 'inner parent' makes more life-affirming choices rather than my 'inner child' doing what it wants whilst disregarding the consequences. As self-awareness increases, we notice the effect different foods have on our system. For instance, when I became a mum I started bloating and gaining weight. Since I was trying to digest the psychological shift from maiden to mother, my physical digestion become more sensitive and I had to concede I could not tolerate gluten. I later found I could tolerate ancient grains, like spelt and khorasan, which meant I wasn't limited to eating gluten free foods that tasted like cardboard. Then in 1997 I stopped being able to digest pork. In 2012 I stopped being able to digest red meat and a year later I felt intuitively it was time to give up chicken - although I did make the exception and have free-range turkey on Xmas Day. I have O Positive Blood, the paleolithic bloodline, so I still eat fish. I find the best fuel for my system is fish, nuts, eggs and plant based proteins with lots of veggies.

We're all different with different abilities to assimilate various substances so it's important we really listen to our bodies, rather than just impose some 'off the shelf' diet plan that someone devised 'cause there is not a one-size fits all prescriptive for our health and nutrition. We are the best ones to intuit what is right for our system. For our body has a conscious intelligence within every cell. We can literally attune to our body consciousness by simply looking at a meal and know whether it's what we need. Those who are more kinesethic (clear sensing), may prefer to place their hand over the food to sense it's frequency by perceiving the energy of certain foods. We unconsciously check-in with our bodies every time we peruse a menu and get a sense of what our body needs. We may over-ride that sense by going for something which we know isn't good for us if the desire is strong enough, but usually there is a moment when we acknowledge what our body would prefer.

Last Summer vacation... we were at a family friendly arts festival and my daughter requested Butter Chicken curry for dinner from one of the market stalls. She ate a couple of mouthfuls then apologized and said she couldn't eat any more. I was disappointed to have spent $10 on it and have it wasted, so I offered it to my teenage step-son son who gobbled it down after his own meal. Everyone who ate the Butter Chicken had diarrhea, including my step-son. I commended my daughter on listening to her body and apologized to my step-son!

So today you are going to listen to your body before preparing or eating any food. Doing this consciously will help you respond to what will make your body happy. Happy body, happy life. If you've got some spare time I thoroughly recommend watching the movie, 'That Sugar Film' which is guaranteed to inspire you to clean up your dietary choices. Here's the link:

https://www.youtube.com/watch?v=6uaWekLrilY

Below I've included what I've found works for me in creating a happier body. Read my suggestions below and take note of what sits well with you and what doesn't. If it resonates, give it a try - if it doesn't, listen to your body, for the body never lies.

— EAT REGULAR PROTEIN. Eating protein at regular intervals throughout the day prevents our blood sugar dropping which creates feelings of anxiety and can lead to emotional outbursts. So ensure you carry some nuts with you (if you're not allergic) at all times to alleviate this. Protein alleviates hunger, so if you're hungry reach for a high protein snack rather than carbohydrates which only fill you temporarily, spiking then dropping your blood sugar levels. Carbs also break down as sugars which undermine immune function and create a breeding ground for fungal infections. Most processed foods contain sugar as well as chemical additives so are best to avoid completely. This includes protein bars and shakes which often contain additives.

— EAT SEASONALLY TO AID DIGESTION. There is a huge push to eat raw, which is fine if you live in a hot climate like Hawaii or Bali but not so appropriate if you live somewhere where you experience the four seasons. In traditional Chinese medicine it is suggested to eat lots of raw salad veggies in Summer. These are packed with raw enzymes (life force) so they energize and hydrate us. Raw foods do take more energy to digest, so in the colder months we need to conserve our energy as the solar light wanes and the days shorten. So too, raw foods are not ideal if you feel run down, suffer poor digestion or feel ill. It is easier for us to digest home-cooked soups, slow cooked meals and curries. Eating raw foods in cold weather can create 'inner damp' resulting in excess mucus in the body. This is even more so if you have a lot of water in your natal birth chart. Eat lots of fresh ginger (steeped in boiling water or cooked in food) in the changing months of Spring and Autumn (Fall) to stimulate digestion, a function which is akin to an engine in our physical body. Eating seasonally is also cheaper as foods can be sourced locally, avoiding them being picked early and put in cold storage for export.

— GROW YOUR OWN HERBS. Herbs are the original drugstores! So do consider growing some near your kitchen for easy access. Most are hardy and make any meal sing! You will also save heaps on pre-packed herbs and herbal teas. They can be ground in a mortal and pestle to make sauces and dressings, steeped in teas, added to soups, curries and salads. Start with the the herbs which feature in your favorite cuisines, then branch out by learning about the culinary and medicinal uses of herbs. You may find it helps to have a poster listing their uses on the inside of your pantry door.

— EAT LOTS OF VEGGIES. Veggies are a natural source of fibre, vitamins and minerals. I have read that ideally every meal should contain 50-60% veggies. I always buy fresh veggies and if possible, organic or biodynamic. Try to eat more greens than starchy veggies such as potato, sweet potato and corn. Steam rather than boil your vegetables so they maintain their nutrients and where possible cook them with their skin on to ensure you get all the vitamins.

— REGULARLY CLEANSE. Every day I brush my skin before getting in the shower to promote the excretion of toxins through the skin. This takes pressure off the lymph nodes, kidneys and liver. I start my day with lemon juice in room temperature water and try to drink two litres a day, along with Dandelion coffee which supports the function of the liver. I also brush my tongue when I clean my teeth to remove bacteria and toxins. Once or twice a year it's great to do a cleanse to help our body to run more efficiently (like having a car service.). This is best done around the Spring or Autumn Equinox as the energy is really high and balanced. That's March 21-23 and September 21-23. I also recommend the book, 'The 3-Day Energy Fast' by Pamela Serure which contains juice and broth recipes along with meditation and processes ideal for a three day retreat to detox body, mind and soul. I also find it helpful to kick-start the process with digestive enzime supplements and probiotics.

— GENERATE BODY HEAT TO ACCELERATE HEALING. Another great manual for self-care is 'Cellular Awakening' by Barbara Wren. She explains how acute episodes of illnesses help rid the body of toxins, so rather than medicating to suppress symptoms, we can support out body's elimination process through the three stages of healing. If ill, raise the core temperature to accelerate an illness through your system faster. Fever is the body's way of purifying toxicity, so if you feel cold and flu symptoms ingest hot drinks and food with warming spices like cloves and cinnamon, which are anti-fungal and anti-bacterial, as well as chili and ginger. Take warm baths and rest in bed with a hot water bottle. This will accentuate the symptoms temporarily but reduce the time of illness.

–   COOK WITH LOVING INTENT. I work from home so I'm blessed to be able to ensure my food is cooked with love. If I don't have the energy to cook, I create a 'no cook' dinner such as a platter of salad veggies with olives, hummus, tuna, smoked salmon or a boiled egg. If I cook when I feel 'burnt out' I usually burn the food or it just tastes terrible because I don't have the creative energy to cook. If I'm in the city I like to go to the Hare Krishna restaurant to eat a cheap meal cooked with love or at a festival I'll seek out the kitchen with the most happy, zen people serving and cooking. I have a saying, 'the best meal is a home-cooked meal that you didn't cook'.

–   EAT WHOLEFOODS. I try to eat wholefoods rather than processed foods as they offer more nutrients than something which looks good, but isn't. I recall watching a show on TV that explained how store bought chocolate biscuits contained blue food coloring. Here I was as a mum not allowing my daughter to eat blue lollies and we were still ingesting the same chemicals used in 'blue loo' cleaners without realizing.

–   AVOID ADDITIVES. I don't eat additives like aspartame and MSG (Monosodium Glutamate). There's lots of literature about how harmful these are. I also use a herbal and mineral toothpaste containing no sodium laurel-sulphate or fluoride (which calcifieshe pineal gland.) Most storebought seasoning mixes contain these flavor enhancers so I'll read the ingredients of the packet and make a note of the spices, so I can recreate it at home but know exactly what's in it.

–   EAT ALKALINE FOODS. I try to eat more alkaline foods than acid producing foods. Meat and dairy foods create acidity in the body, which increase the likelihood of us experiencing emotions like anger and having a system more prone to illness.

Whereas alkaline foods, such as plant-based foods alkalize the body, promoting calm emotions and physical health. Instead of meat, I eat fish which is full of omega-3 fatty acids which are great for many functions in our total health and wellbeing. Several studies have found the omega-3s in fish are great for easing depression. One study of fifty-two pregnant women found that taking a 300 mg capsule of omega-3s during pregnancy significantly reduced the women's risk of postpartum depression.

Good nutrition minimizes mood swings and lessens comfort eating. It is one of the ways we nurture ourselves in a practical way so we feel supported, care for and loved.

DAY 10: HAPPINESS HABIT

GET A 'FEEL GOOD' HIT BY GIVING

Scientific studies show people who volunteer to assist others, live longer and experience less illness. This is because we give meaning to our lives when we make a difference. The more direct our involvement, the more we see the positive impact resulting from our actions and this helps us to feel connected to something greater. Giving to those in need of assistance also helps put our own personal challenges into perspective. Without this broader outlook we can become insular and see our problems as insurmountable and drown in self-pity.

Experiencing the direct impact of you help through volunteering is also far more rewarding than merely donating to a charity and there are limitless opportunities to respond all around us to those in need. Through personally knowing the worth of our contribution, we generate a feeling of pride in our efforts. This builds our self-esteem and enhances our self-image, which is crucial if we are to feel happy about who we are and the life we are living.

Traditionally in our modern-day culture, it has been the third age members of our community who have done the most volunteering. This is because they have the time and many want to actively continue to make a contribution to society. Many parents also volunteer as part of their children's education and extra- curricular activities. This may involve spending time assisting with working bees, camps, concerts, coaching and fund-raising. Volunteering is, however an important practice for us at any age, regardless of our social situation. In fact, it is an essential part of raising well-rounded adults that we ensure our youth experience the benefits of volunteering. This helps tweens, teens and twenty- somethings gain a broader understanding of life beyond their personal circumstances. This is essential if they are to gain a sense of personal responsibility as global citizens, so they don't remain a children psychologically, focusing solely on their own needs and feeling indignant if they don't always get what they want. Given the degree to which kids are subjected to high budget Hollywood films, celebrity envy, product placement in films and constant advertising which targets them through all their high tech devices, it is imperative that we, as a collective community of adults ensure they are exposed to what lies beyond the virtual world and are actively invited to participate in making a difference.

This is particularly important when we consider how vulnerable our youth are to experiencing bouts of anxiety and depression. Whilst integrating their inevitable loss of innocence as their become increasingly aware of the shadow side of life, both personally and in the world they see around them they can feel overwhelmed and powerless. It is these mental health conditions that form a fertile ground for habitual drug and alcohol use as a way of escaping and numbing their sense of hopelessness and despair.

As a result, many under the age of thirty will experience suicidal tendencies if they cut from adult support in their need to rebel against the adult world who they hold accountable for their dysfunctional world. Growing cynicism is often fueled by a sense of paralysis to affect any real change, along with personal self-doubt about one's own potential. Volunteering offers an opportunity to shift that negative spiral.

In the Hindu tradition, the monkey-God, Hanuman made the transition from being a mere mortal to a God by dedicating himself to being of service to others. This is also why saints have traditionally been honored as divine vessels. By asking that we be used for the greater good, we awaken the soul which un-taps our true genius...and there's one inside of everyone, each uniquely talented.

So rather than military service, I would love to see our youths encouraged to become involved in community service projects that make a positive difference in the world as part of their education. Fortunately many schools are now incorporating partnership ventures with aid agencies, where high school students are encouraged to work part-time to raise the funds needed to travel to developing countries where they take part in a good works project.

In eastern philosophies this path of service to others is known as 'Dharma'. Dharma means, 'that which contains and upholds the cosmos'. Dharma means ensures justice is carried out through right action which assists all living beings and not just oneself. Dharma is love in action, ensuring human life is sustained, in harmony with nature. I have experienced the power of Dharma in my own life. In fact, what kept me going in my twenties when I felt disillusioned with life, was a project I tried to create for eleven years called, *Good Morning Unemployed*. (A TV show designed to assist those feeling disenfranchised with humor, practical tips and inspiration to become self-employed ethical entrepreneurs.) When that show was turned down by ABC TV I plummeted into a severe depression. It was then I discovered ancient women's wisdom and customs and devoted my life to helping women empower themselves. Then at age forty-four I found myself deeply disturbed when I realized the degree to which girls and women were marginalized and suffering in the developing world. This awareness came from reading the book, *Half the Sky* by Nobel prize winners Nicholas D. Kristof and Sheryl Wudunn. I cried for two days because I felt powerless to help girls as young as eleven being sold into a life of sexual slavery. My daughter was the same age as these girls who every day were subjected to multiple rapes, life threatening sexually transmitted diseases and induced drug abuse. I read the book in response to being asked by Atira Tan, (founder of the Art2Healing Project), to train women to facilitate women's rite of passage ceremonies and monthly Red Tent sharing circles. This type of work was sought after as she found it restored the sense of sacred sovereignty that the habitual abuse had destroyed. After speaking with Atira about how I could help, I was lit up like a Christmas tree in gratitude to her for having set up a structure whereby I could directly make a difference to these women's lives. In the months that have followed, despite our plan to travel to Nepal in September of 2015 being postponed due to two large scale earthquakes, I devoted myself to writing and launching this book and organizing an awareness raising speaking tour with Atira in the UK. This was only possible due to the women who signed up for my course to learn how to facilitate Red Tent women's circles in their local communities, some of whom have donated funds from their circles to Art2Healing and organized their fund-raising projects such as art exhibitions. As a result of my involvement with Atira's foundation in the past few months I have noticed how my response when people ask me how I am is usually, *'Happy'*. I have Atira to thank for this...and you for buying this book!

CALL TO ACTION

We are now in the Aquarian Age. The two thousand year window when, as a collective, we learn to embody the lesson of the most altruistic sign - Aquarius.

That makes this the optimal time to consider how you can contribute to the whole for the betterment for our global family. So today is the day to ask, 'What can I do to make a difference?' Keep in mind that whatever you commit to must feel inspiring, personally rewarding and even fun!

So it's helpful to consider these two things:

1. Who you would most like to help.

2. The skills and natural aptitudes you have.

You may like to draw upon your own life experience to provide support that you wish had been there for you. For example:

I wrote my first book, *'The Inner Goddess Makeover'* after I discovered the empowering map of feminine archetypes which helped me understand and empower my feminine sense of self. I wrote it as a gift to all my sisters as I felt it was every woman's birth rite and I wanted to offer more support than I had felt as a young woman, with a lack of positive role models and guidance.

I created the Red Tent online course as a structure to create more support for women, especially single mums who were growing exponentially and needed more support if they were to sustain themselves and support their kids on all levels. This was borne out of my own desperation as a single mum.

So here's today challenge...

STEP ONE: Think about a sector of the community whose plight troubles you, angers you or saddens you. Focusing on it may increase your feelings of despair or anxiety in the short-term - however, not acknowledging the degree to which it upsets you maintains a continual low-level continued stress. If there's more than one, write them all down then circle the one that jumps out the most.

STEP TWO: Write down all the skills and qualities you have, such as compassionate listening, gardening, drawing, singing, baking, blogging, knitting, photography, networking and then circle the one you love to do the most.

STEP THREE: Now ask your inner self - your soul who accesses your infinite intelligence, to grant you inspiration to make a difference to the lives of those people you care about, using your fave gifts and skills. Close your eyes and see what thoughts, ideas, memories or visions surface or occupy your mind. If you draw a blank, try opening your eyes and doodling with a pen on paper to free up the 90% mind to daydream without interruptions from your 10% rational mind.

You might serve a sector in your local community or those who you see as having a real need on a global scale. Take note of any thoughts of friends, family members or acquaintances who come to mind, as they might collaborate with you in some way.

Please Note: DO be realistic about the time you have to commit to helping others as the aim is not to try and become so altruistic that you martyr yourself for a cause. You may only do two hours in a soup kitchen once a year on Xmas Day, but it's still a huge gift to those less fortunate, which will enhance everything else you do. So rainbow warrior - choose your battles. Select one cause and focus on making a difference there, rather than trying to be all things to all people and spreading yourself too thinly.

DAY 11: HAPPINESS HABIT

EXPRESS YOURSELF WITH CREATIVE PLAY

Most people upon entering a kindergarten will feel uplifted. This is because the room is filled with dozens of bright, multi-colored artworks created from a place of innocence. They are not critically acclaimed works, they are simply done as honest and spontaneous outpourings of feelings and experiments with different media.

Oftentimes it is this naive art that moves us more than the great works. This is because the focus is not upon perfecting a craft, with the viewer in mind. As a result, we respond to children's art from our feelings and our sense of innocence, rather than from our own discerning, yet critical mind.

Art is after all, the language of the soul. That is the function of art and why it is imperative to our wellbeing as a shared humanity. Expressing ourselves creatively requires we consult the inner self, shifting the focus from our everyday thoughts to what desires to be expressed through us. Whether we see ourselves as creatively gifted is irrelevant.

Art enables the soul to feel recognized, heard and expressed, which is why it is used as a powerful therapy to help people reconnect with themselves and their deepest feelings. It has been proven to be one of the most effective techniques to assist those recovering from trauma, even when the trauma is endemic and handed down from one generation to the next. 'Art play' is a form of meditation which helps still our mind, focusing upon what is present and alive in us, emotionally and psychologically. It enables us to acknowledge what is unresolved within us, which restores inner calm through a sense of personal validation of our truth.

So today is an invitation to have a date with your innocence. To express yourself with no judgement, simply for the experience of pure self-expression. The result is not important.

CALL TO ACTION

To do this activity you will need to gather some tactile media. You don't need to go to an art supplies store - your pantry will be sufficient.

Here are some ideas:

- Google a play dough recipe and make some play dough on the stove. Then make shapes or whatever comes to mind. Then smash it and make something else. The impermanence helps us to move past any 'shoulds' we're holding on to in our lives, along with any attachment to what outcome our ego would've liked in situations that still retain anger or resentment when we think of them.

- If you have acrylic paints, squeeze out some blobs and use your fingers to make patterns or squirt the tubes on a sheet of paper, like Pro Hart.

- Scatter some flour on a flat surface, (like your kitchen bench). Then draw something and rub out your drawing and start over as many times as you like, using your fingers.

- Make a mandala on the floor, table or a tray using crystals or uncooked pasta.

- Play with your food! Fashion some edible art, such as a necklaceout of sweets, a face out of veggies or a sculpture out of fruit. (Toothpicks can be used to hold your structure together!)

You may like to invite big kids or small kids to join you! In fact, if you didn't manage to come up with a way of volunteering in the previous chapter, this may be an opportunity to take someone else's kids for a few hours to give them a few hours to themselves. You may have so much fun, you may make a monthly or seasonal date out of it - helping a neighbor, family member or friend in need. This is the ultimate gift you can give to a sole parent! For more great ideas, here's the link to a wonderful blog site with lots of wonderful ideas for creative play:

http://artfulparent.com/kids-arts-crafts-activities-500-fun...

DAY 12: HAPPINESS HABIT

BE 100% AUTHENTIC

When we suppress our true thoughts and feelings - who we really are inside, we reject parts of ourselves in order to fit in, to help others feel more comfortable or to avoid the potential pain of being rejected by others.

Exactly what we suppress to fit in or appear socially acceptable will be different for each person. For example, for some their challenge will be finding the self-worth and courage to say, 'No' more often than they say 'Yes' to others in order to break a pattern of over-committing. This is often done to appease the endless wants and needs of others, resulting in feelings of resentment and exhaustion.

For others - especially if you live in a small town, you may find it hard to individuate from the one social group you're expected to mix with, rather than opt for spending time alone or with one other person, for fear of being ridiculed by the dominant social group. Ultimately, we will each inevitably get to a point where we have to be honest with ourselves about whose company uplifts us and whose company drains us. When we acknowledge this to ourselves, it is a natural progression to review our choices. Then we spend less time with people who we don't have much in common with. Similarly, we will not place pressure upon ourselves to indulge the company of those who bring us down with their negative outlook, their limited world view or their need to put others down as a way of unconsciously bolstering their own self- esteem.

As your personal empowerment grows, you may decide to stop going to ball games, if they bore you, just to please your family. Instead you will seek out other activities you can genuinely enjoy doing together. You may limit the number of functions you attend with your partner's family, rather than going out of a sense of duty or obligation. and with your free time seek out a hobby you've always wanted to try or enjoy some quality alone time, reading a good book. For others, being 100% authentic may mean daring to plan a trip of a lifetime on their own or with a friend, which holds no interest for their partner or family.

Some of you may question how the persona you project to the outside world does not accurately convey who you really are. For example, you may attempt to hide your age by wearing a toupee or dying your hair to cover your grey hair, for fear of being rejected for looking older. We may think this a harmless concession to make, given it's so commonplace. However, when we really consider we are rejecting who we really are in order to please others, we may gradually welcome back our 'silver hairs' as a sign of personal power and wisdom.

If we hide who we really are - such as never admitting we have different values or spiritual, political views to our parents, or becoming a doctor, lawyer or engineer because it's the expected career trajectory, rather than follow our own passions, we will die a bit inside each day, as our facade takes more and more energy to maintain. When I worked in the courts I was struck by how many barristers showed severe signs of premature aging.

Compare that to living an authentic life, where we dare to be who we are at home, when we're out in the world, so our outer reality matches our inner truth. This way of living decreases our stress levels, as our sense of acceptance comes from within, rather than gauging how acceptable we are to others. When our locus of reality is internal, we accept that not everyone will understand who we are and why we make the choices we do. However, the chance of drawing those who do resonate with our choices is far greater when we live a transparent life.

What inspired this post was an image I saw of a cake someone baked to give to their parents as a way of 'breaking the ice' with love and humor, in revealing their homosexuality, thus avoiding a potentially confronting conversation all round. As a heterosexual woman I have not lived through the torment of revealing my gender preference to my parents but I'm glad there are blogs like this to inspire people to do it sooner rather than later, and with love. (By the way, it's worth clicking on the image to read the letter next to the cake in one of the images of a 'coming out' cake. It's a gem.)

http://www.buzzfeed.com/hnigatu/24-awesomely-creative- ways-to-come-out-of-the-closet#.ryBoWxoOM

CALL TO ACTION

If you're still looking for your soul mate or your soul clan - those who truly see and celebrate you, for who you are, dare to try this challenge and make being authentic a daily habit.

For the next twenty-four hours, make only authentic choices. To do this, consider every invitation, request or opportunity that people make via email, on social media, at home, work, school - even at the supermarket check-out....if they ask, 'How are you?' respond authentically. For example, 'I'm feeling tired /

impatient / frustrated or insular' and watch how this opens the possibility for much more meaningful connections with complete strangers, as well as your friends and family. Sure, some may not know how to handle your honesty if they haven't yet found that courage themselves, but many will find it so refreshing to connect with someone who's really up for some genuine interaction, that you'll find you get great service and find new levels of connection with people you may not have found previously.

So look for opportunities to be completely honest, using tact and considering the feelings of others in how you respond, but not to the point of compromising your truth to accommodate them. The more you risk being you, the more your inner self will shine! Start with small decisions, where the stakes are low, and before long this practice will create a life where you feel excited to wake up every day because you feel aligned with your deepest truth in all the choices you make. Then your life is truly your own.

Should you falter, for fear of what others may say or do...read this poem aloud. Then once more with feeling! (Yes, it's the one made famous by that wonderful film featuring the eternal light of, Robin Williams, *Dead Poet's Society*.)

INVICTUS

By William Ernest Henley

Out of the night that covers me,
Black as the pit from pole to pole,
I thank whatever gods may be
For my unconquerable soul.

In the fell clutch of circumstance
I have not winced nor cried aloud.
Under the bludgeonings of chance
My head is bloody, but unbowed.

Beyond this place of wrath and tears
Looms but the Horror of the shade,

And yet the menace of the years
Finds and shall find me unafraid.

It matters not how strait the gate,
How charged with punishments the scroll,
I am the master of my fate,
I am the captain of my soul.

DAY 13: HAPPINESS HABIT

CULTIVATE SOMA: THE ELIXIR OF BEAUTY

Soma is an ancient Tantric word. It refers to the essence of life we extract from moments of beauty and pleasure. Described as a 'Vedic ritual drink', some have misunderstood it to be a physical brew, distilled as a euphoric herb. It is in fact, the energy of pleasure we drink into our being through our physical senses. The word, Soma simply means 'body' as distinct from the emotions, mind or psyche (soul).

Many of us have been conditioned to have a conflicted relationship with our bodies and our physical senses, viewing them as something we must not trust or indulge in, lest we get carried away and forget our minds completely. However, if we are to be truly happy, we need to love and appreciate every aspect of ourselves and our life around us, by seeing and experiencing the divine in it all. That includes honoring the sensual realm through our physical senses with reverence for all the wonders they grant us access to. Appreciating our need for Soma ensures we take the time to 'smell the roses' and feed ourselves through our sensate reality. This means taking life in through all our physical senses; sight, smell, touch, taste and hearing - and through them appreciating the goodness life has to offer.

There are two ways we can cultivate soma. One is through pleasure and the other is through beauty. Pleasure does not have to be limited to supreme indulgences like sipping hazelnut liqueur while soaking in a warm milk and honey bath. Rather, it means being available to the simple pleasures sensate communion offers us, such as walking barefoot on soft, fresh grass or fine, silken, grains of sand or digging your hands into rich and fertile soil.

It's allowing yourself to notice and deeply inhale the smell of freshly baked bread when walking past a patisserie or smelling your partner's skin when you turn over in bed.

Beauty is said to be in the eye of the beholder. This is because beauty is ever present but only seen by those who attune their perspective to notice it. When we live with a heightened awareness of beauty, we see it everywhere, which uplifts our soul. Like the scene in the film, 'American Beauty' where the young film maker admires the dance of a plastic bag in the wind - rather than merely judging it with the rational mind as litter, followed by a tirade about the state of the world. Beauty gently affirms that life is worth living. That for all our human struggles there are moments of transcendence, which fill up our senses.

Beauty reminds us the Divine is omnipresent. It is only when we turn away by attuning to our clocks, schedules and agendas that we lose touch with the free gifts of providence that are all around us, waiting for us to notice. For when we become busy and preoccupied in our heads, we no longer see from our hearts through the eyes of our soul. From the mind's perspective we see ourselves, others and everything around us as a series of problems that need to be fixed and attended to. Understandably, this leads to feelings of overwhelm to which we often respond by hardening our heart as a coping mechanism. When this response becomes a habit, we exist in a state of cynical numbness, leaving us unavailable to the juiciness of life.

WHY WE NEED SOMA

Soma is the ultimate anti-stress agent. It's why people are so keen to go on holiday...it's usually the only time they make the time to fill up on soma! Yet given the amount of stressors we encounter constantly in our modern lives, we can't underestimate the importance of ensuring we increase the amount of soma we gift to ourselves on a daily basis, to alleviate the build-up of stressors we are exposed to.

Stress is a state of inner hysteria which occurs when we deny the needs of the inner self or Soul, which is feminine, regardless of our physical gender. In our high-tech modern lives it is easy to fall into a habit of always being, 'on' where we feel constantly available to respond to emails, texts, mobile phone calls, Skype messages and calls, Facebook messages and notifications. This places our attention in our minds, which makes a mental note of all the things we need to attend to, which we're exposed to. Understandably, the mind becomes overwound with the relentless input of data. Just as overwinding a piece of string causes it to become tight and inflexible, so too, our mind becomes rigid and we become increasingly tense and unable to respond in a flexible way to unexpected outcomes if we don't take time to unwind. Soothing the feminine part of us through the sensual pleasure is the key. I speak about this in more detail in this video:

https://www.youtube.com/watch?v=3t_ysP-l1D4

So soma is the antidote for an overwrought mind. It is through attuning to the senses that we come back into our bodies. This helps balance our energy from being completely focused in the head, which leads to neck pain, sinus congestion and headaches and distributes it throughout our entire body. Soma focuses all our awareness on the area of sensate pleasure being stimulated, so it is a form of Earthly meditation - a state of heightened awareness. It is what sex therapists prescribe for people who are so disconnected from their bodies that they have no libido. For if we aren't connected to our own bodies, we can't attune to the subtle sensations of another's. Loving life through the senses also helps us to become more loving in general. For we are more likely to connect physically with those around us through loving touch, if we are not setting ourselves apart like a brain in a jar, who views those around them as a problem to be solved rather than a gift to be appreciated.

CULTURAL CONDITIONING OF SOMA

Those in the East, the feminine cultures learn how to cultivate soma as a way of life from their early childhood. They witness the adults in their community exchanging massages, giving herbal treatments to each other's bodies and sharing sacred beauty treatments using natural ingredients sourced from their local surroundings. This is why, despite their apparent lack of modern- day conveniences, people seem genuinely happier and more relaxed in many developing nations, compared with those in the West who have appear to have everything they could possibly need struggle to feel happy.

Whereas those in the West, conditioned by a more masculine culture, often are taught to spend time acquiring knowledge and skills, rather than connecting sensually with those around them. Such a focus is more oriented to being indoors and utilizing technology than perceiving the natural world through the earthly senses. So is it any wonder we grow up to achieve, but struggle with feelings of anxiety and depression, which impacts upon our personal relationships and personal happiness?

ANOTHER GREAT REASON TO CULTIVATE SOMA

Just as particles transform when heated up, so do we. In addition to global warming heating Earth's atmosphere from the release of carbon emissions, we are experiencing a quickening of the electro-magnetic waves of energy around the Earth. This phenomena is called Schumann's resonance. It is created through a build-up of energy created between the positive charge of the Earth's ionosphere and the negative charge of the Earth's surface. In December 2012 we entered the band of electromagnetic particles called the Photon Belt, otherwise known as the 'Rings of Alcyon'. (Alcyon is the central star within the Pleiades star system, also known as the Great Central Sun.)This influx of light is positively charging the ionosphere, creating a hothouse for us to bloom into our next evolutionary phase, as beings with a multi-dimensional awareness.

So things are hotting up here on Earth in more ways than one. You can see this mirrored in both world events and our daily lives. This makes it especially important we learn to regularly partake of soma, the 'happy elixir' as a way of harmoniously integrating the effect of Mother Earth's quickening electromagnetic frequencies. So never dismiss the need for a massage as a frivolous indulgence, as it is now a necessity for ensuring you don't experience the following symptoms of electromagnetic stress:

— migraine headaches

— impatience

— mental confusion

— feeling irritated and quick to anger

— extreme tiredness

— muscle cramps

— electrical sensations in the limbs and spinal column

— flu like symptoms

Another symptom of electro-magnetic stress is when we find ourselves stressing about time. This is because time is literally speeding up. This can lead us to try and get more done in smaller amounts of time, leading to an amplification of our stress levels. This results in more emotional outbursts as people literally crack under the inner pressure, which adds to the stress levels of those who witness and receive their distress. The good news is all of this is awakening our kundalini, our 'inner fire' which accelerates and expands our awareness. Think of a mustard seed being dry roasted in a pain, till they crack open and transform or metal being heated in a crucible in the ancient art of alchemy. For more info on how to support your inner alchemy during these pivotal times, including how to raise your own frequency to match the rising vibration of the Earth, through kundalini teachings and practices check out my book, 'Creating Sacred Union Within'. (See Resources.)

CALL TO ACTION

DRINK IN THE ELIXIR OF SOMA

Today, look for opportunities to be fully alive in your senses - not just one, but all of your senses. Here are some suggestions...

SMELL: Remember the feeling that permeated your whole being when you last inhaled the scent of an old-fashioned rose? See if there's a nursery or garden stocking 'Double-Delight' roses nearby or a pharmacy that stocks essential oils or a perfume counter stocking the scent of tea rose or rose absolute. Then go and stick your snout in one and inhale deeply and notice if you feel all tension within dissolve. Alternately, light some good quality incense that makes you purr or smell some ground clove or cinnamon from your kitchen pantry. Breathe the sensation of pleasure into every cell to feed them with soma.

SIGHT: Look up and notice the palette of colors in the morning sky, the dew on a spider's web or the way the light refracts into rainbows on your kitchen floor. Breathe this moment of beauty into your entire being so that every particle within you smiles.

SOUND: Listen to children laughing, birdsong outside your window or the sound of wind rustling through leaves.

TASTE: Bite into a fresh mango, peach or cherry and allow yourself to really murmur and thoroughly enjoy the sensation of its taste.

TOUCH: Wear clothes that feel divine on your skin and are so enticing that others can't help but reach out and touch them, such as fabrics which feel soft and silky or fluffy and soft. You may wish to treat yourself to a sheepskin rug to sit on naked in front of a fire so every part of your body can enjoy the sensate arousal of titillation as you move around like a happy cat. Do be sure to release your pleasure through sound, to release any pent up stress.

I would also like to share this song and video clip with you to remind you that you are beloved and a part of something that is precious beyond words. You are part of the sensual majesty of pulsating life. So make the time to feel the sacredness of pleasure through all your senses.

https://www.youtube.com/watch?v=uGi490LmaP8

DAY 14: HAPPINESS HABIT

ENGAGE IN ACTS OF SILLY DISOBEDIENCE

If you had the words, 'Stop being silly' spoken to you often as a child, chances are you've fallen out of the habit of regularly being silly. This is a sad state of affairs and one that will turn you into a very dull and grey member of society if you don't take immediate action.

We have so many rules imposed upon us to ensure we all act appropriately in our roles as professionals, parents, spouses, upstanding citizens, responsible neighbors, dutiful daughters and diligent sons, so it can feel truly liberating (to both ourselves and others) to be deliberately inappropriate, in the name of good fun. (This is why comedians have jobs - to release the valve for those who do not dare rock the boat or risk making a fool of themselves on a regular basis.) However being a voyeur of comedy will not give you the same release as being a complete idiot yourself.

In my youth I worked as a stand-up comic and as part of my act I would ask the audience to stand, hold up one hand and make the following pledge, *'I promise to spread silliness and naughtiness wherever there is danger of life being taken too seriously. Noo ne Noo!'* You are welcome to adopt this pledge in your own workplace, home, neighborhood or community center in the hope of rousing more people to join you in doing something silly.

In the film, 'Happy' they say statistics show exercise releases even more endorphins when we add a pinch of silly to it, such as the annual footrace where people dress in gorilla suits. Personally I recommend playing totem tennis in over-sized gumboots (also known as wellingtons or galoshes) to give everyone an even handicap.

CALL TO ACTION

Today you are going to do something silly. It may be something on your own, such as putting slices of pastrami in your shoes (a la comic, Steve Martin) guaranteed to make you feel silly throughout your day or you may inspire others to join you in your ridiculous escapade to help them to lighten up! If attempting to inspire work colleagues to join you in doing something silly, such as a walk in the city mall dressed as tree frogs you'll probably have more success if you plan this in advance. This will give them time to get their head around it and inspire them to do it as a dare.

You may wish to do something silly now, to get you in the mood - such as wearing your clothes back-to-front while you post your silly event idea on Facebook inviting your friends to do the same and upload their photo as their form of acceptance. The more people you rope in the better and they will all be grateful to you for helping to free their silly which may not have had a day out in years!

Here are some of my silly tips:

- Try pogo spring-loaded boots (avail for hire in some cities)
- Attend a trampoline center with pits filled with foam pieces you can jump into
- Dress up as waiters and serve cucumber sandwiches and sparkling apple juice to motorists when they stop at the traffic lights (I did this complete with a violinist to serenade them)
- Deliver a singing telegram that you wrote yourself dressed in costume
- Round up your office staff for a jog around the block in your lunchtime wearing silly hats
- Make a novelty car or add a novelty wind-up attachment to your roof if you drive a mini as your contribution to reducing road rage
- Wear a red nose or grouch marx mask on the train home and act normally
- Wear your underpants on your head (if you have an afro like I did as a child you can pull your hair out of the leg holes to make teddy bear ears)
- Serve up dinner in face formations
- Ask everyone to join with you in singing in operatic voices for an hour so everything said must be sung instead of spoken

Here's more ideas on a website funded by the UK government:
http://www.bureauofsillyideas.com/

DAY 15: HAPPINESS HABIT

FEED YOUR MIND WITH INSPIRATION

The mind is like a double-edged sword. It is a wonderful tool for analysis, discerning all the stimuli we're exposed to, but like everything, it needs to grow. If we don't regularly feed our mind with concepts that expand our perspective, it can turn in on itself with self-criticism and paralyzing over-analysis, resulting in self- doubt.

Once we get into a negative head-space, we can spiral into a labyrinth of limiting stories and beliefs which evoke heavy emotions, such as fear, guilt, despair and resentment. So to keep your mind positive and light, fill it with bright ideas which inspire growth. It might be as simple as turning off the TV or computer and having a designated night to read on a regular basis - which is a great way to unwind before sleep. Or you may wish to enroll in a short course or full-time study.

One British study by the Office for National Statistics found that the higher people's level of general education, the more satisfied they were with their daily life, and the more worthwhile they felt. More than fifteen thousand people were surveyed to rate how satisfied they felt overall and how worthwhile they felt their lives were, on a scale from one to ten. Eighty-one percent of those who said seven out of ten or higher had the highest level of education. The numbers fell in accordance with their level of education.

So if you didn't know what you wanted to do when you left school and fell into a job which now thoroughly bores you, take steps to pursue something else. Maybe you used to enjoy your work but have grown tired of it as it no longer holds a challenge. Dare to contemplate what spikes your curiosity. You may wish to start with a short course. Many are online and part-time, making them easy to incorporate into our lives.

Learning something new, be it through reading books or doing classes, adds another dimension to who we are. It gives us the ability to connect with people out of our usual sphere, enhancing our social skills when we attend social gatherings. It also helps give us something new to speak about with our partner and often enables us to connect more deeply with another member of our family who shares an interest in that subject.

Nowadays with the internet, there is information on every suject imaginable at the touch of a button. However, there is still a great pleasure in visiting your local library to thumb through books on subjects that normally you wouldn't think to search for, which may catch your eye and capture your interest.

The more we nurture our minds, with interesting subject matter, the less we think and talk about petty issues, such as what the neighbors are doing. Illustrated beautifully by this quote by Eleanor Roosevelt:

'Great minds discuss ideas, average minds discuss events and small minds discuss other people.'

THE POWER OF A FRESH PERSPECTIVE

Reading inspirational quotes and affirmations helps raise our thoughts above the mundane concerns of our everyday world. Given all change begins with a thought, a fresh perspective may have life-changing consequences. This has been one of the lovely aspects of online social networks, with many people sharing daily words of inspiration. Every day I also post a free message of inspiration on my Facebook page and I have an app so you get daily notifications on your phone when it goes live. (See Resources.)

Discussing your challenges with someone who can provide wise counsel can also help move us out of a negative self-talk loop. If you prefer a more clinical approach, seek out a recommended psychologist but if you prefer a more holistic approach, seek out a psychotherapist, transpersonal or intuitive counsellor. If you only want a one-off session to address a specific challenge, try an intuitive oracle reader who can help shed light on your problems from a higher perspective, by identifying your soul lesson in a given situation. (Do be discerning and trust your own intuition with any professionals you entrust with your mental health, regardless of which sector in the industry they work. Where possible, ask friends for referrals and do not give your personal inner authority over to them, remembering they are there to serve you, so there is no obligation on your part to keep seeing them if you do not feel their assistance is helpful.)

Another way of shifting old limiting beliefs is to participate in a personal development workshop or retreat. These are usually intensive events offering the designated time and skilled facilitation to process issues that may have been causing ongoing stress, consciously or unconsciously (evident by behaviors such as compulsive worry or teeth grinding.) They often catalyze a turning point in participant's lives, providing them with the impetus to make big life changes. For it is often our own passivity, due to a fear of change, that leads to feelings of powerlessness and depression. So having someone inspire us to make the shift from an external locus of reality; blaming, making excuses and feeling victimized to an inner locus of reality, assuming ownership and taking responsibility through pro-activity, creates huge positive changes in a short amount of time. As always, be discerning and trust your first sense about someone, regardless of their hype.

MAINTAIN YOUR OWN MIND

Teachers are really helpful in accelerating our understanding. However, we must ensure our intuition remains our highest authority figure at all times. This prevents us from handing our personal responsibility over to a third party, such as a charismatic teacher, leader or group mind that seems to have everything we've been looking for. No one person has all the answers and any good teacher will encourage you to grow beyond them rather than engendering dependance. So be mindful if you encounter any group that uses techniques to break down your ego such as sleep deprivation, asks for any kind of submission to their group mind, requires that you tithe your income to them, complete levels of training that cost increasing amounts of money or takes audiences into regressed states then uses the NLP phrase, 'By now you will have realized' - encoding the words 'buy now'. Above all, trust what your body tells you and your first impressions, as they are never wrong.

ADDRESSING THE ROOT CAUSE

If you find, despite your pro-active steps to read books, do courses and have private sessions that you still create patterns of self-sabotage, you probably have some deep-seated negative beliefs in your sub-conscious mind needing to be addressed. Hypnotherapists are a great resource for this and often all you need is one to three sessions to clear an issue. It involves taking you into a really relaxed state and addressing the subconscious directly to get to the root of the problem.

Another way of working with the sub-conscious is through creative visualization. Creative visualization is ancient manifestation technique brought to mainstream awareness by Wallace Wattles (1860-1911) who wrote, 'The Science of Getting

Rich'. It involves focusing on your heart's deepest desires as vivid images in your mind's eye (imagination) with a sense of deep gratitude. This magnetizes to us what we do want rather than focusing on worries which unconsciously attract to us what we don't want. This is a technique used by Olympic athletes to entrain both their minds and muscles for success, with credible results.

Finally, be discerning about the media you expose your psyche to, as the sub-conscious mind cannot tell the difference between real and virtual experiences, resulting in unnecessary trauma for the mind to process if you watch violent films and the news channels. Watching events that shock and dismay us, leave us feeling powerless, inducing stress. News reports are also unbalanced, as they focus on the worst events of the day, which generates feelings of pessimism. Great things are happening all around the world, so attune your dial to those affecting positive change and you'll feel much better.

CALL TO ACTION

Today do one of the following things, then consider how you can incorporate some of the other suggestions listed:

- Seek out a quote for the day to inspire you. You may like to keep a book of affirmations or inspirational quotes beside your bed and read one every morning to start your day or find something quotable online.

- Visit your library and borrow non-fiction books on lots of interesting subjects and great fiction books you can lose yourself in to relax your mind.

- Don't watch or read the daily news.

- Read an inspirational autobiographies about someone you admire, as this will reassure the mind that everyone has challenges, and they can be overcome.

- Check-out courses, classes, workshops or retreats that excite you to learn.

- Don't occupy your mind with gossip, as this pre-occupies the mind with comparisons which are debilitating.

DAY 16: HAPPINESS HABIT

LOVE THY NEIGHBOR

I am very fortunate to have great neighbors. I often speak about how thankful I am to have the world's best landlord living next door. I called him 'The Patron Saint of Single Mothers' as he took a chance on my five year old daughter and I, after we'd been homeless for a year. (He had always made a practice of renting his second house out to single mums when a lot of landlords had a prejudice.)

We have a very symbiotic relationship. It works well as we help each other out by doing what we're happy doing, which the other needs. For example, he loves doing yard work and I love cooking, so we exchange. There is no hidden agenda, just doing what comes naturally, with an awareness of self and other.

When we are vulnerable we reach out for community. Cultivating a sense of community makes life easier for everyone as it helps us to restore the balance. For example, in our modern lives, some of us are time poor but asset rich, whilst others have time, but are short on funds. So all we need to do is be more open to collaborating and dare to put forward a proposition to enrich the lives of both with additional support.

Take a moment to notice if someone intuitively pops into your head in response to this idea, such as a neighbor or someone else in your community, then follow the lead to explore opportunities for exchange. We are here to learn to live together because the truth is, we need each other. We are all vulnerable in some way - competent at some things and less so at others, so consider how you can live more co-operatively with the folk fate has surrounded you with.

CALL TO ACTION

Have a read through my tips for cultivating a great community spirit in your neighborhood...then choose one to action today!

GET TO KNOW THEM

If you haven't connected with your neighbors to date - consider having a street or block party. Put invitations in everyone's mailboxes and ask them to bring a plate of food to share. This might be the start of something beautiful!

WELCOME NEW NEIGHBORS

It may take less than an hour, but can make a world of difference to someone who has uprooted and stepped into the unknown of a new location. I usually bake something and stop by to welcome new neighbors. If you don't bake, you may want to take a bottle of wine or pick some wildflowers.

SHARE YOUR RESOURCES

We exchange clothes and toys we no longer use that are in good condition and we swap and share utensils and ingredients for baking, as needed. This is really handy when you find you need one item and don't want to drive to the supermarket in the middle of baking!

DO YARD WORK

If you are able-bodied or have kids who are and you have an elderly, disabled or depressed neighbor, consider cleaning up their yard, without asking for payment. It is important our kids learn the importance of a good deed and not always expect a monetary exchange for everything they do. Paying it forward promotes something far more precious than money. In my case, my landlord cuts free firewood for us, as this helps him keep the block fire safe which gives us a free energy source. He also does all our yard maintenance, such as burn-off's and pruning. His adult son (who lives above him with his wife and two young kids) blows the leaves from our drive when he does his. He also mows our yard and once a year gets on the roof and cleans our gutters. (I give him German beers in gratitude!)

COOK A LITTLE EXTRA FOR SINGLE NEIGHBORS

If you love to cook, consider who around you could use a home-cooked meal made with love. One woman who took us in when we were homeless had her ninety year old neighbor over for dinner every Monday night. I cook meals for my landlord. He is a single middle-aged man who is so grateful for regular home-cooked meals. It is no extra trouble to make enough for him and I enjoy nurturing him to express my gratitude for his kindness. I have also taken frozen left-overs to a local single mum who I knew was struggling with depression.

KEEP EACH OTHER SAFE

Think about how you can look out for each other. Whether that's being available to your neighbor's kids till they get home from work or texting them if there are hail stone warnings so they can ensure their car is under cover. For example, whenever there is a high fire danger day (for bushfires) my landlord comes over to warn us to leave the mountain in the morning. I have a phone app for high risk day notifications so I'm not just dependent on him, but I'm always touched by his care and concern and the human contact is lovely. In the days when I was seeing private clients for intuitive oracle readings, if I had a new male client whose vibe I felt unsure about, I would let him know and he would walk past and check everything was okay.

CARE FOR EACH OTHER WHEN SICK

When my landlord has had the flu, I've offered to buy him groceries and make him soup. When we have had gastro or viruses I've texted his family to ensure they stay away so their kids don't get sick.

TAKE OUT THE GARBAGE

My landlord does this every week because we share our bins - which is great because we always have enough room between us. So consider opening a conversation with your neighbors about sharing bins, so if you have a party you know you can use the empty space in theirs. Or if you have a neighbor, who is time poor or recovering from surgery, you offer to do this chore for them.

HOLD THEIR MAIL / NEIGHBORHOOD WATCH

Whenever we go away we let my landlord and his family know, so they keep an eye on our place. We ask the local post office to hold our mail, so he's not burdened with that, but it's a nice thing to offer to do if a neighbor is going away for a short trip.

BE NICE TO THEIR PLANTS, KIDS AND PETS

Offer to water their plants if they are sick or going away. My landlord bought a bunch of hand-picked flowers off my daughter and her friend (from his own garden) to support their entrepreneurial ingenuity. We make sure we buy sweets at Halloween for local kids coming to 'trick or treat'. His daughter-in- law babysat my daughter once a week for free before she had kids so I could go to Kabbalah class when I was a single mum. (She had been raised by a single mum so understood firsthand our need for community support and the lack of funds for paid childcare.) We have looked for their dog when she got lost and we always welcome Mika, the dog with pats and treats and have prayed for her when she ate a bait and got bitten by a snake.

BE SUPPORTIVE OF THEIR WORK / DREAMS

When I used to have full moon gatherings here every month with a community

 dinner, my landlord next door never complained about the crowds. If I had a client coming for a reading and he started up with his whipper snipper, I would explain I had a client coming and he would cease for that duration.

I have bought computer parts off him and crafts off his daughter-in-law and loaned her tables for her to put her wares on at craft markets and given her paper bags to sell her stock in. We take an interest in the growth of each other's endeavors, encouraging and affirming their efforts. Another neighbor who was recovering from an induced coma after severe pneumonia had lost her ability to paint and was a gifted artist. So I arranged to have a photographer take images of her art, then researched how to create an online gallery for her after she had allowed me an extended payment plan to buy one of her paintings for my 40th birthday. She has made a full recovery and relocated and we are still friends.

ACKNOWLEDGE THEIR MILESTONES

If a neighbor has a baby or a birthday its lovely to mark the occasion. We have always been invited to first birthday parties and my daughter was even asked to be the flower girl for my neighbor's wedding. My neighbor also donated and planted a flowering peach tree over my daughter's buried placenta which we'd carried with us for five years until we found a safe place to plant it. I have baked cakes for their birthdays and we have been invited to share breakfast on Christmas morning. I give them Christmas gifts. They're not expensive, often home-baked goods. I've also given them flowers to celebrate the start of Spring, which were on special at the local greengrocers.

DAY 17: HAPPINESS HABIT

THE JOY OF A SHARED TABLE

In our hectic daily lives it can be all to easy to eat on the run, while walking down the street, driving in our cars, while talking on the phone, working at the computer, watching TV or standing at the kitchen bench multi-tasking. If we consider that the more attention we bring to our food, the more it will fulfill us, none of these are wise practices. Standing, walking or being distracted while eating is also bad for our digestion. Similarly, if we eat food while watching TV, we are swallowing all those images as we try to digest our meal - giving ourselves an overload to digest and often these a negative images and sounds we're being subjected to without warning.

The ancient gnostics use to always eat in silence so they could bring their full awareness to the act of communion, in appreciation for the gift of life which sustained them. This was then continued by those who lived in religious orders. This is a great practice to try, especially if you're on retreat or doing a health cleanse, but for everyday living it robs us of a wonderful opportunity to catch up on the day with our closest and dearest.

SETTING THE SCENE FOR COMMUNION

By sitting around a shared table, we set the scene for interaction. Whereas when we sit side-by-side facing the TV there is little opportunity for reading body language, facial expressions and hearing each other over the dominance of the television. (This lack of family cohesion is depicted beautifully in the film of Roald Dahl's, 'Madeline')

So too, if we take the time to change the tablecloth, put on placemats and add a small vase of flowers from the garden and light a candle, we create a visual invitation which says, 'You are loved and welcome to dine'. It is perhaps even more important to do this if we live alone so eating doesn't just become a perfunctory task, like filling up the car with petrol. This is why many singles eat out in cafes so at least they are around other people while they eat. Fortunately, many cafes now have communal bench seats and long tables to encourage people to connect. Even if they don't, it's nice to offer to share a table if you see someone eating alone who isn't giving out vibes that they'd rather be left alone. I once shared a table with a woman who asked when I was in a busy cafe and she ended up hosting me as a guest in a resort in Bali so be open to possibilities!

As a sole parent I used to find mealtimes became a chore when we sat at the table, as I spent most of my time policing table manners as the only adult present. Whereas when I started sharing meals with other single parents, we all enjoyed our mealtimes much more. We'd either take turns to cook or both bring a plate to contribute.

Community is created through the regular act of communion. Communion is the act of coming together with the intent to share. It is an intrinsic human need. This is why indigenous cultures like the Australian aborigines don't have a word for 'thank-you', as it's a given that one shares what they have, in a spirit of oneness. Sharing a meal was the original act of communion. So regardless of our spiritual or philosophical beliefs, we can enjoy a sense of deep connection through sharing meals with friends, family and those we feel intuitively guided to extend an invitation to.

Every meal is a sacred act if we stop to consider:

- how fortunate we are to have food to eat

- the effort put in by those who grew, harvested, transported, sold and prepared the food

- the sacrifice of the living entities being consumed so our life force can be sustained (Note: even vegetables have a consciousness - watch the yoghurt spike the stress meter in the film, 'I Am' for further confirmation.)

So when we take a moment to acknowledge the energy that has gone into our meal, we come into a state of oneness with all who have been a part of the life force we are ingesting. This brings us into a harmonic alignment with the molecules of the food. This assists digestion and the assimilation of nutrients and creates an act of communion, even if we are eating alone.

There is no one way to enter into this state of communion with your food..

- some bow their heads and pray to a Father God

- some sing to the Earth Mother, elements and Father Sun

- some chant Y-AH-M the Sanskrit sound that opens the heart center

– some Reiki their food, sending unconditional love energy via their palms

– others eat in silence

– some murmur loudly with ecstatic pleasure and burp loudly to express their joy and gratitude

All that matters is our intent. When we 'break bread' with friends, family, loved ones and strangers, we share this act of communion with the all. Eating is an intimate act. When we share a meal with someone we have the opportunity to really relax and get to know each other, which is why a meal is the social ritual for both romantic dates and business deals. This is why the act of giving food to someone who is hungry or welcoming them into your home for a meal is such a powerful act of oneness, as it affirms you have considered for a moment what it would be like to be in their shoes and such kinship is heart-opening for both parties.

Sunday lunch used to be a family tradition in the West, where Christian families would gather after church to share a roasted animal and vegetables. As many of us grow up and pursue careers in locations distant from our family of origin, this tradition has waned and now seems to occur predominantly in small farming communities. Similarly, Jewish families set aside Friday evening as the beginning of the Sabbat (holy day) when the family gathers for dinner. Nowadays this is a tradition seen more amongst orthodox families who walk to each others homes for their Friday night dinner. Muslim families feast together at the end of Ramadan, the holy month of fasting during daylight hours in a spirit of oneness. However it is not uncommon to share the one platter during meals rather than having separate plates, which is a far more communal act of dining than having separate plates and less washing up! For Mexican 'Day of the Dead', families gather and cook the meals of their grandparents, sharing their wisdom and stories as they set a place for their ancestors to join them in spirit, through the aromas of the dishes prepared.

In the West, it is often immigrants from the more feminine cultures who still honor the tradition of gathering with extended family to eat on weekends. This is based on my own observance, as whenever I visit places of natural beauty, I am always touched by how many Indian, Maori, Sri Lankan and Samoan extended families are there together enjoying a BBQ or picnic, indicating how much sharing a regular meal, is a valued part of their culture.

Similarly, my partner's family, who are French speaking Belgium natives also value family feasts with lovely china and glassware.

Perhaps my favorite historic act of communion was enacted by the elite French holy order of Cordon Bleu knights, made up of blue bloods accustomed to fine nosh who each bore the blue ribbon of chivalry. Legend has it, they met in secret to express their worship of the divine through the creativity they put into the elaborate dishes, which they would bring as offerings. This is where the style of 'Cordon Bleu' cooking originated. (I learned that tidbit sitting in on a court case when I worked as a court reporter in a case between the Cordon Bleu cookery school and a canned pate company.)

So if any of you have been lucky enough to share a meal with French folk, the act of eating for them is an elaborate ritual, a sacred affair with attention to detail in many small courses - each matched with a different wine and served on starched linen, silverware and crystal glassware. (I'm sure not every French person eats like this. I'm basing it on a lunch I shared with French natives my sister used to dance with at the Moulin Rouge.) More importantly nothing is rushed. The entire afternoon is dedicated to exchanging ones intimate thoughts and feelings, over shared sensual pleasures. Similarly, the Italians renowned for their long lunches 'al fresco' with family and friends sharing good food, wine and laughter.

CALL TO ACTION

So consider reawakening this time-honored tradition of sharing a meal on a regular basis. Whether you take it in turns to host or work your way through different cuisines. Cook with love, serve with love and enjoy the soul fulfillment of a shared table. I did this once for thirty people on Christmas day - an 'orphan's Christmas' comprising of people who chose not to spend it with their family of origin and it is still one of my fondest memories.

Here's a few suggestions to choose from to anchor this happiness habit! If organizing a shared meal, try to set it up on a cyclic basis and maybe take turns hosting to spread the responsibility of cleaning house.

WAYS TO CREATE MORE CONNECTION AT THE MEAL TABLE

- Take it in turns to go round the table and ask everyone the highlight and lowlight of their day. This gives those who are less talkative a chance to be heard!
- Involve others in laying a nice table, and encourage them to use their creativity to make it inviting.

–   Turn off the TV, don't allow phones at the table and put on lovely music to dine with.

— Consider who you know might be interested in sharing cooking / eating once a week.

— Invite someone to share your table at a cafe.

— Try blessing your meal before eating - have fun with it!

— Try eating a meal in complete silence, to be in a state of complete mindfulness with every mouthful of how lucky you are to have food to eat.

— Organize a monthly community dinner on the weekend closest to full moon and invite everyone to bring a plate of food to share (I stayed with a family in my final year of college who had a tradition one Sunday a month where all the men would cook.)

— Plan a Sunday lunch with family or friends, as a picnic, at home or at a local restaurant.

— Sit down for all of your meals to aid digestion for this day on.

— Add fresh flowers and a candle to your table for ambiance or splurge on some new placements, a bright tablecloths and napkins.

DAY 18: HAPPINESS HABIT

EARLY TO BED, EARLY TO RISE

I have always been a night owl. As a child I used to sit at my window and sing to the moon. Then in my twenties I worked as a performer which meant coming alive at night. In my thirties I became a mother...and night time became 'my time'. It was when I had the headspace to begin my 'second shift' - working at home after I put my daughter to bed. I did that for years until chronic fatigue slapped me around the adrenals like a wet cod.

To help shift my sleeping pattern and become a morning person I created a *'Sun Worship Challenge'* on my Moon Woman Facebook page. This meant I would have to be accountable, not just to myself, but to all the people who joined me in committing to attune their body clock to the dawn.

The first change I made was to implement a settling routine, as one would for a small child. This was to give my mind a chance to unwind before going to bed, instead of just closing the lid on my laptop's bright screen and expecting myself to instantly fall asleep. (Kind of like slamming on the handbrake in the middle of a busy intersection.) So I made a rule to unplug from all screens at 9pm so I could go to bed at 10pm and wake at 6am. On the mornings I slept in past the alarm I noticed I was grumpy, quick to swing into martyrdom and desperate for my first swig of English breakfast tea. Whereas the mornings where I journaled my dreams, meditated and exercised, I felt centered, positive and generous of Spirit. (I often found I wouldn't have my first cup of tea till mid-morning!)

Please understand, I'm not suggesting you stay home and knit every night and don't attend parties, ball games, films, theater or art exhibitions, if they finish late. I just know how much better I feel when late nights are the exception, rather than the rule. For when we rise with the sun, we access the natural energy source of solar light to power us through our day. This means we start to wind down as the sun sets, ensuring we are ready to sleep before the lunar energies rise to their zenith between 10pm and 2am, which is what keeps insomniacs awake till the energy wanes at 2am.

Ultimately, if we live against the natural cycles, doing what is unnatural, it will eventually catch up with us. So the sooner we acknowledge we need to rise with the sun to feel brighter energetically, psychologically and emotionally, the easier our life becomes and the happier we are.

For those of you who have seen the film, '*Happy*' you may recall the island in Japan with the highest number of people aged over one hundred. One of the reasons they gave for this phenomena was their early bed time which enabled them to weed their gardens every morning before breakfast, providing them with morning exercise. One doesn't have to look far to notice elders the world over, retire early and rise early, to walk or garden. If we concede that the older we live, the more we learn, it stands to reason that over time we figure this out for ourselves.

Until then, the bright lights of social media and television beckon us like moths to override our biorhythms - in case we 'miss out on something' so we stay up late, like naughty children and bolster ourselves with a shot of caffeine in the morning to mimic 'The Force'.

For those of you overwhelmed by responsibilities, trying to multi-task within an inch of your lives, try rising early to get things done, instead of doing your tasks late at night. Make this golden hour or two, your 'me time' - tending to your needs, before tending to the needs of everyone else, be it your family or work. This will anchor support from the 'get go' so you are less likely to feed stories of victim / martyrdom.

'Early to bed, early to rise, makes a man healthy, wealthy and wise.'
Benjamin Franklin

CALL TO ACTION

- State your intent to become a morning person on your Facebook page or tell your friends, family or housemates so they can support you in your intent.

- Write down all the reasons you would benefit from being a morning person. The more reasons you have, the more inspired you'll be to keep going, even if you slip up one day. You may wish to pin this on the fridge or next to your bed.

- Google the time of sun rise in your location and set you alarm. (Sleep cycle app can help you set a time so you wake up at the end of a sleep cycle and don't feel like road kill!)

– Put a journal and pen beside your bed and an MP3 player if you want to be able to meditate sitting up in bed with headphones.

– Upon waking, Write down any dream symbols and how you felt in your dream.

– Meditate for 15 mins. I've created morning meditations to ground, energize and balance in my good Morning Chakra Workout double CD which you can also download as an album or single MP3 tracks. (See Resources)

– Do some gentle stretching. I like to do a mix of yoga and pilates poses.

– Exercise for 30 mins before you start your day - outside if possible in nature. If the weather's not inviting put on some music and dance in the lounge room! (Kids can join in.)

DAY 19: HAPPINESS HABIT

CLEAR YOUR CLUTTER

As stated before, all matter is made up of vibrating energy, so when we collect a lot of stuff around us that we don't really need or use, we surround ourselves with stagnant energy. Energy which doesn't move, holds our past low emotional states, such as sadness and anger, making it harder for us to let go of old situations which no longer serve us. So clearing clutter helps us to thrive, rather than just exist. Since our home environment reflects the state of our consciousness, we often have a messy house when we feel chaotic inside. However, the opposite is also true. When our house is disorganized, we find it harder to think clearly. If this sounds far- fetched, try telling a child to get ready for school when their room's a mess! Children are especially sensitive to energies, but it's a phenomenon which affects us all.

Usually people keep their clutter as a form of security, like a child building a fort - a domain where they can shut out the outside world and feel safe and justified in protecting their insecurities. When we hoard objects from the past, it keeps us attached to and invested in the past. Whereas, when we sort through our stuff and discern what to keep and what to move on, it affords us the opportunity to reflect upon the feelings and memories associated with each object. By just keeping everything tucked away, we don't allow ourselves the chance to really feel, acknowledge our endings and move on. This inaction passively affirms our future won't be any better than what we had in our past...which becomes a self-fulfilling prophecy, if we don't clear a space for new opportunities to come in.

Karen Kingston's book, '*Clear Your Clutter*' is a great resource if you are prone to clinging to the past. The one piece of advice I recall from her book is simply to ask yourself, 'Does this object arouse a positive or negative response in me?' This is the fastest way to discern what stays and what goes so your sanctuary only contains objects which raise your energy with positive associations. So if you've been given a gift that you don't like, that you're keeping for show should the gift-giver come a knockin' - get rid of it.

I'm not suggesting you discard photos of deceased pets and family members, but maybe instead of having the entire house as a shrine to them, have an altar of remembrance that you tend to with fresh flowers each week, rather than having them look at you from every corner of the house. A great habit to adopt is to use the seasons of change, Spring and Autumn (Fall) to clear your clutter regularly so you don't end up with a 'room of shame' that everything gets dumped in.

If you're someone who finds it hard to let go, 'in case one day you might use it' or because you see the value in it and don't want it to be wasted, then give it to someone who'll use it more than you, on the proviso if you need it, you can borrow it.

Where possible, recycle by offering what you no longer use to neighbors, relatives, friends, thrift shops, advertise on an online bulletin board or have a garage / yard sale so you can see how happy people are to take your once loved items to a good home, where they'll be appreciated. Since every object has a consciousness, a vibration which oscillates at a vibration too dense for our retina to detect, I like to take a moment to thank each object that journeyed with me and wish it well on its journey.

This is where the term 'Indian giver' originated. The Native Americans acknowledge every aspect of creation has a destiny to fulfill, so if they hold on to an item that they aren't using, it doesn't honoring it's highest purpose. So during the times of the early settlers, if a native American intuited an object needed to move on and wasn't being re-gifted, they would ask for it back, so they could assist it on its journey.

When we give away items, we affirm through this action that we will receive whatever we truly need, when we need it, by not hogging the energy ball of abundance. So release what you no longer use with reverence, welcoming in the breath of Spirit to surprise you with serendipity.

CALL TO ACTION

STEP ONE: Today think of one item you own which you don't use and consider if there's anyone you know who might use it. If you can't think of anyone, then give it to an opportunity / thrift shop.

STEP TWO: Make a date on your calendar to sort through a section of clutter in your life. You may wish to start with one box, rather than overwhelm yourself with a whole room. Let the success of one box inspire you to do another box and so on.

If you share your home with others, offer them an incentive to join you in clearing out their clutter. With kids, this helps them to recognize one stage of their life is over by giving away toys and clothes they once loved. You may invite them to do a yard sale where the profits will go towards doing something really fun together.

DAY 20: HAPPINESS HABIT

CREATE SACRED SPACE

This suggestion deliberately follows on from clearing your clutter. For when we get clear on what we don't want, it's easier to identify what we do want. When we let go of the past, we also create a void to fill with objects that represent who we are now and what we wish to consciously call into our lives. For our home reflects back to us what we choose to surround ourselves with. It's a physical affirmation of what we're welcoming in. This is why Feng Shui experts advise that we put up images of us looking happy with our favorite people, rather than the artwork, *'The Scream'* in our bedroom if we want to ensure harmonious relationships!

A HOUSE IS NOT A HOME

Our home is either a sacred space or just somewhere we hang out hat, depending on the amount of love we invest in it. A sacred space is a sanctuary in which we can feel relaxed enough to feel safe and nurtured. This encourages us to reconnect with our inner self and truly feel 'at home' so we can center, process and replenish our energies. Our home is the container that holds us, when we feel scattered or depleted. So the more we take time to make our home environment a sacred space, the more gracefully we will navigate through whatever challenges we encounter in our outer world.

THE POWER OF INTENT

A sacred space can be both a physical temple space which honors the preciousness of life and the quality time we gift to ourselves to be a human 'being' rather than a human 'doing'. We have more chance of setting this time aside on a regular basis, if we set the space for it. In the film, *'Field of Dreams'* the protagonist played by Kevin Costner, builds a baseball field on this premise, 'Build it and they will come'. So too, if we create a sanctuary for our soul to find peace and inner contentment, we create the fertile ground for that intent to manifest.

TAKE ME HIGHER

In addition to creating a nice ambiance, we can really raise the frequency of our living space by creating a designated sacred space. This may be a table or shelves on which we place objects which remind us of the sacredness of life or a room or corner where we mediate or do yoga. When we create an intentional sacred space within one part of our home, it raises the vibration of the whole building, elevating it to that of a 'temple space'. That means all who enter feel uplifted and walk away feeling better for having visited. In addition, our home resonates at a higher vibration, which helps us to rise above problems and view them from a higher perspective.

Many homes in ancient cultures had a designated space to spend in contemplation. Today Taoist families still have a temple space in their home, where they bless fruit at new moon and Hindu families in Bali have an outdoor garden shrine, where they make ornate offerings every dawn and dusk.

HOW TO CREATE A SACRED SPACE

Have a designated welcome area with a small altar featuring an object of natural beauty and either a sign inviting people to please remove their shoes before entering or a shoe stand next to a quote, prayer or poem which affirms your philosophy for living. By stating this at the entrance to your home, you are setting an intentional boundary, asking all who enter to honor this is a place intended to be in alignment with those values. For example, at the entrance to our home I have a wall banner with the words:

I honor the place in you where Spirit lives.

I honor the place in you which is of Love, of Truth, of Light, of Peace

When you are in that place in you

And I am in that place in me, Then

we are One.

Ultimately a sacred space has a focus which affirms love. Love of self, other and the all. Many people create this intuitively in their home when they care about where they live. The more strongly we state this, the higher the wattage of good vibes - so long as it doesn't become 'holier than thou' then we've lost the point as people will tiptoe in and whisper for fear of doing something wrong.

I'm not a feng shui expert but I feel intent is more powerful than any system we may learn. So in my home I create some kind of altar in every room, in keeping with the elemental energy and intent of that room. For example, I set objects to inspire sacred bathing water rituals in the bathroom and Tantric artwork and candles in the bedroom to inspire soulful union. That way every room we enter reflects back to us that we are a divine emanation in physical form, which makes it easier to make choices accordingly.

Creating altars is a very calming activity which creates sacred space within us as we focus upon creating that intent externally. Children often do this intuitively in their rooms, arranging their special objects carefully on their shelves. They also love to be involved in creating seasonal altars with found objects from walks in the entrance to their home.

It is very important to keep your altar spaces as clean and tidy as possible, as these are spaces which carry a heightened intent. So if your special shelf or table is covered with dust, flowers that have seen better days and your crystals are dull from never seeing the sun - make it a priority to give them a spruce.

CALL TO ACTION

Today you are going to create a sacred space somewhere in your home. A sacred space will look different to each of us, depending on the philosophical path that calls our soul. It also depends on how much space you have to work with. So consider what part of your home - inside or outside you could create a truly uplifting sanctuary to return to, when you feel scattered, broken or depleted...and even when you don't.

Here are some suggestions to inspire you:
- create a labyrinth (a simple maze marked with stones which you walk as a meditation with a place of contemplation in the center))
- water features (such as a lotus plant in a pot or a goldfish pond)

    —statues (of nature devas, totem animals, Gods and Goddess archetypes, spiritual masters, bodisatvas, saints and teachers)

- artworks and photographs of natural beauty that elevates the soul

- quotes, words or affirmations

- candles, lanterns and essential oil infusers

- crystals

- a chair, mat, cushion and blanket for meditation or yoga

- plant a rose garden or a mandala herb garden

- create a shrine of remembrance to a loved one with photos or plant a tree

- make a zen garden with river stones or sand which you rake to still the mind

- gather natural found objects and use coloured cloths to create a seasonal altar

- erect a tipi - this may even be done with a mosquito net inside as a quiet place to sit

- create your own mandalas with ribbon, beads, seeds and crystals

DAY 21: HAPPINESS HABIT

CAST THE BURDEN

You have probably heard the saying, 'energy flows where attention goes' meaning what we focus on, we give energy too. This is why it is counterproductive to worry, for ourselves or another, as our negative projections feed the possible scenarios we're hoping to avoid.

The rational mind is a powerful tool, like a computer. It's great at analyzing and troubleshooting, but it doesn't have access to all the data, which the higher mind does intuitively. So we must learn to discern between the two. The higher mind is subtle, so only perceived by us, if we awaken the ability to witnesses our rational thoughts. When we awaken this inner witness, we can observe our intuitive responses (the initial thought or sense we receive) then use the rational mind to organize our needs in accordance with our intuitive guidance. If we override the more subtle inner voice with the constant demands of the rational mind, we become enslaved to it's incessant stream of data and become manic, like a machine with no sleep mode.

The role of the rational mind is to troubleshoot and problem solve. So once it identifies a potential problem, often based on previous experience, it projects the worst case scenario into the future as a potential hazard in order to deduce a pre-emptive strike. If it can't determine a suitable course of action to alleviate potential harm, it can become preoccupied with a particular situation until it assesses it as solved.

Some situations in life can't be immediately solved - not in accordance with our preferred outcome. In such situations, all we can do is adjust our attitude by considering the situation from a different perspective. In order to do this we must first free the mind from its fixation. To do this I recommend a practice which is in many philosophical paths. It's called, 'Casting the Burden'.

It is done by simply handing whatever problem the mind is wrestling with, over to the benevolent, infinite intelligence to solve

- thus freeing the rational mind from the burden of finding a solution. This is, in fact, the most logical approach, as the rational mind does not have access to the big picture, including all the unseen variables. So it cannot determine the optimal outcome, due to it doesn't have all the facts on which to base its assessment.

Whether you ascribe to quantum physics or a holistic worldview, it is arrogant to think that we, alone have all the answers. Especially when some of the world's great thinkers ascribe flashes of inspiration to some of their greatest breakthroughs and ideas. So by actively inviting the infinite intelligence of the Universe to participate, we avail ourselves to a much larger resource of ideas. This practice is also referred to as 'co-creation'. It honors the fact that we can create something great in isolation, but if we invite the unknowable force of highest will and synchronicity in to assist us, we end up with something far greater than we imagined. It will also manifest with a lot more grace than struggle. When we co-create, we humbly acknowledge that our rational faculty is inherently limited because it doesn't know the limit of its own ignorance. Put simply, 'it doesn't know, what it doesn't know'.

So if we get to an impass, a wise and humble soul will surrender the solution to highest will. A less graceful soul will persist stubbornly trying to work it out on their own, often at a great personal cost to themselves and those closest to them. This is because the way the rational mind solves a problem is through anaylsis. This can lead one into a wormhole of complexity, when the truth is often elegantly simple. In fact the rational mind will often entertain so many possibilities from an unlimited number of angles that it will go round in circles, to the point of complete paralysis. It is usually only when we give up, that the answer comes in an unexpected moment, when we're focusing on something else, such as standing in the shower, when the mind is freed of intently trying to solve the problem.

CALL TO ACTION

Today you're going to 'CAST THE BURDEN'! So take a moment to think of something that's been taking up room in your frontal lobe. Something your mind has been tossing backwards and forth, perhaps the last thing you think about before going to sleep or the first thing you think about whenever you wake.

STEP ONE: Identify the problem and acknowledging that the unknowable quotient is causing stress, since you don't have access to all the facts (such as future influences).

STEP TWO: Invoke a higher power to take the burden of trying to solve your given situation. For example, 'Highest truth, I surrender up to you, (name the situation) to highest will for the highest good of all.'

STEP THREE: Every time your mind goes back to try and nut out a solution, affirm the situation is being resolved in accordance with highest will.

Should your 'monkey mind' start in on you with reasons why this isn't a proven method, here's something to chew on; surrender is not an act of blind faith. Surrendering to the infinite intelligence of the Universe is based on deep awareness that the Universe is far greater than the sum of our rational thoughts. This expanded awareness restores the beautiful mind to a state of grace, so it may function and serve us better.

DAY 22: HAPPINESS HABIT

THE SPIRIT OF ADVENTURE

You've no doubt heard the quote by Heraclitus, "Change is the only constant in life." This is because we are made up of moving particles of energy and energy is never still, it is always in flux. Large, dense forms of energy change slowly over thousands of years like eroding cliff faces, whilst more delicate life forms, like a butterfly move through a complete life cycle in a maximum of eight weeks.

How much we grow depends on how much we embrace change. Yet so many people fear change. Change is only scary if we don't trust our inner selves to cope with whatever unknown challenges may come our way. However, it is through embracing the unknown that we discover inner qualities like self-reliance, ingenuity and resourcefulness. The longer we resist change the harder it becomes, whereas when we give ourselves small challenges to move beyond familiar territory, we build our confidence to take greater risks. Those who dare to keep moving beyond their comfort zone learn firsthand, 'variety is the spice of life'.

To embrace life fully, we need to love life. In other words, our love of trying new experiences must exceed our fear of what could possibly go wrong. This means being heart-centered, rather than mind-centered. If we consider we are either growing or decaying, spiraling up in ascension or spiraling down in entropy, the only real option is to 'choose life' to quote singer, George Michael. One of the ways we can CHOOSE LIFE is through the spirit of adventure.

To do that, I recommend that each year you go somewhere, or do something you've never done before. It doesn't have to be a death defying, thrill-seeking sport like base jumping, but entertaining an adventurous intent will help get you thinking out side your box and exploring possibilities for living a larger life. For example, if there's a country you would like to visit, but for various reasons feel unable to travel there in the immediate future, research if there are any cultural festivals, social clubs or restaurants to sample that culture without boarding a plane. Similarly, you may dismiss all adventure sports if you are confined to a wheelchair. However, there are many organizations committed to assisting people with physical impairments to scuba dive, which could literally open a whole new world!

You may wish to ask every member of your inner circle, what their greatest adventure would be. If incorporating children of different ages, ask everyone to make suggestions inclusive of all. You may find it helpful to offer a list of suggestions, such as going to Disneyland, hot air ballooning, holidaying in a horse-drawn gypsy caravan, swimming with dolphins or going to a tropical island. Then do a private vote, with each person writing down or drawing their preference. Alternatively, leave it to fate and pull one out of a hat.

When everyone is part of the brainstorming and decision- making, they feel empowered with a shared sense of ownership and are more likely to be willing to be actively involved in helping to make it happen. When everyone is on board from the inception, you can then formulate a plan to make it happen, whereby everyone contributes, no matter how big or small. This gives kids an experience of taking a vision, which feels like an impossible dream and creating a step-by-step strategy. It also means kids aren't in a passive role, expecting others to give them everything on a platter without having to work for it themselves. It also teaches them rewards are so much sweeter when you've had to put in some effort to achieve them. Next, have a brainstorming session around the table with large sheets of paper and colored textas and to write down (or draw) all the fund-raising ideas you can think of. This is an opportunity to do something together that can be a truly rewarding shared experience, which bonds you deeply as a group.

This is a great way to encourage kids to work part-time or do more chores at home or for neighbors, friends and family. Each month you can have a round table meeting to review what fund- raising efforts worked and what didn't and celebrate the person who contributed the most to the holiday fund with a reward. These meetings will help you all to see whether you need a one, three or five year plan or whether to adjust your end goal to something more within reach. You may find it helpful to draw a graph depicting the amount you need and colouring in targets reached each month. At these meetings, you can also devise more ways to generate funds, depending on the season, such as carwashes in Summer and raking leaves in the Fall. Suggest big jobs, like cleaning windows and roof gutters, which people need to do once a year and would gladly pay someone else to do. Each person might have a jar with their name on it so they have a visual incentive as they see the jar filling up. This will inspire them to come up with their own creative ways to generate funds. It's also a great way to inspire kids to help out with age appropriate ideas. For example, teenagers may babysit in addition to getting a regular part-time job, or they may be more entrepreneurial and see a need they can help to fill, such as assisting older people to learn how to use social media or download music, using their skills to help another for an hourly rate. Younger kids can help fold flyers and do letterbox drops if they are supervised by an older child or adult. This also gives one leverage for getting big jobs done which don't hold much appeal, since most kids will gladly help clean out the attic, if they think the money from ebay sales will get them to Disneyland!

If you're a sole parent - consider asking another sole parent if they'd like to join forces to have a family holiday. I did this on a couple of occasions and found it so much easier and enjoyable than trying to go it alone! We did it on the cheap, sharing a room together in youth hostels and caravan parks and were eligible for family tickets at holiday attractions.

Having a major event or goal to look forward to acts as a beacon. It's something that lights you up every time you think about it. So you can draw upon this to inspire you as a worthwhile goal when you lack inspiration for the task at hand. This helps create a positive attitude, which is infectious. And the more you share your dream, the more you'll inspire others to do what they can to help you. So rather than turning up for work each day, resentful that all your money seems to go on responsibilities like rent / rates, utilities, transport, insurances, education and medical expenses - it can include helping you make your greatest dream a reality!

Many years ago I read the book, *'Travels'* by Michael Crichton

- the director of the film, *'Jurassic Park'*. He lived this way, planning and pursuing a different adventure every year, for no other reasons, than his curiosity and desire. He then shared some of his adventures in his inspiring book.

Often the things we most want to do, are the things we don't dare think about, let alone try to make happen, for fear of failing and experiencing disappointment but if we never try to live the fullest life imaginable, we only live a half life. So it's worth noting that inspiration is what fuels our life force. If we are not pursuing that which most inspires us, life becomes meaningless and we comfort ourselves with destructive acts of denial such as shopping, over-eating or substance abuse, rather than confront the fears that keep us from pursuing our heart's greatest desires. So if you've felt envious towards those you see as living 'the good life' it's time to make a change.

An adventure does imply risk as taking a step into the unknown will confront you with your fears. However, it is the moving beyond the oppression of a fear, which holds the most exhilarating reward. For instance, you may suffer from xenophobia; a fear of not getting your needs met in another country if you don't speak the language. Acknowledging this fear, helps us take pro- active steps to move beyond it, such as enrolling in classes to learn a foreign language.

A WORD TO THE WISE

If visiting a new place. Talk to people who have been there. You can Google advice forums like 'Trip Advisor' on the place you are planning to visit and get word of mouth from people who have been there. You may also want to post on your Facebook wall that you're thinking about traveling to a specific destination, asking if anyone else has been there and has any advice. Try not to 'over plan' your trip as what's most amazing about taking a magical mystery tour is allowing synchronicity to be your guide. This is easier if you are traveling alone, as a couple or with a friend but not so advisable if you're in a group or with your family. If at all possible, book the first couple of nights in a new destination, then leave it open so you can be available to the spontaneity of who you meet and how they influence your adventure.

When the day arrives to finally depart, as you sit in the plane, bus, train or car, I recommend stating your intent for your adventure to the universe. For example, 'May the forces of love and truth guide me, so I'm always where I'm meant to be, meeting the people and going to the places in accordance with my highest destiny.' When we take action to do something new and exhilarating, despite the risk of getting it wrong, getting hurt or even dying in the pursuit of living life to the full, we honor the gift of life by feeling truly alive, in the moment, and excited on all levels of our being.

CALL TO ACTION

Take a moment to notice how the word, 'adventure' feels inside of you. Is there resistance or enthusiasm? What connotations does that word carry for you? Take a moment to unpack that - write down all the words, memories and feelings that come to mind when you say the word, 'adventure'. Know that adventure means something different to everyone. So your idea of a great adventure will be different to someone else's. For example, if you had Mt Everest on your list of words, but have a fear of heights, remember you get to choose your own adventure. So now you've confronted any self-sabotage, you get to dream of all the experiences your heart desires...

STEP ONE. Write down all the travel destinations that call you - think of the cultures, landmarks, cuisines and landscapes that pique your interest and call your soul. Researching a place you've never visited before or trying something you've always wanted to do is guaranteed to excite you with anticipation.

STEP TWO. Write down all of the experiences you'd like to try - opportunities to study abroad, retreats / ashrams, pilgrimages to sacred sites, scenic hiking trails, cultural events and festivals, adventure sports (such as scuba diving / surfing / sailing / motorcycle riding), animals you'd like to see in the wild, places abroad you would like to volunteer or people you'd like to meet on your family tree.

STEP THREE. Choose the one that most jumps out at you - the one that lights you up with enthusiasm.

STEP FOUR. Research what you would need to make it happen. This affirms to the benevolent universe this is the trajectory you would like to direct your energy into. This mobilizes unseen forces in a myriad of ways to assist you in aligning with your intent.

STEP FIVE. Once you have gathered all the facts, you can formulate a step-by-step plan to achieve your dream and have the time of your life! As suggested, you may wish to invite a friends or family together to brainstorm the ways you can raise the finances needed. Consider having a garage sale, selling what you no longer need or finding second-hand items at garage sales to sell on ebay. Think about the individual and collective skills you have and how you can use those skills to make money, such as hosting a community events like dinners, film nights, exhibitions or talent nights. Think of the sorts of jobs people need done and do a flyer drop or announce to your social networks that you're looking for odd jobs such as babysitting, pruning trees or clearing gutters to save for something you've always dreamed of doing. If you're someone who's done lots of courses but never used your acquired skills, this may give you the impetus to start offering your services, such as healing sessions, Tarot reading at markets, holding art classes for children or baking novelty birthday cakes.

DAY 23: HAPPINESS HABIT

REFLECT UPON AND RESOLVE YOUR EXPERIENCES

If we don't regularly take time to process the experiences we've been exposed to, we can feel overwhelmed by the sense that life has gotten on top of us. However, in our modern culture, we are often affirmed when we are outwardly productive rather than when we stop to contemplate our life lessons. This means we often don't think to make a habit of journalling, recording our thoughts and feelings about past events, which gives us an opportunity to process them.

As a result, it's not uncommon for us to repeat the same destructive patterns. This is a far more costly way to learn, in every sense. In addition to attending to the fall-out, our reaction is magnified by the frustration of past events and self-criticism for repeating a lesson learned. So it's good to get in the habit of doing a regular life review. There are many ways we can do this.

—   JOURNAL WRITING. Having a book you write all your thoughts in, helps to empty the incessant chatter of the mind and get clear. It's a good idea to keep a journal by the bed if you get insomnia, so you can do a 'mind dump' by writing out 'head chatter' so your mind can then let go of the need to try and resolve it then and there. Personally, I feel it's important you don't have such a beautiful journal, that you dare not pen your inane babble. For we often need to write out the shopping list, meal plans and social plans before we get to the real issues which are buried deeper. Having a regular time to journal is optimal, rather than just when you're in crises. I also recommend drawing and doodling in your journal, which is often revealing and cathartic.

Drawing helps free the mind, like a gentle meditation, which allows for inspired ideas to flow from our higher mind. Most of all, write as if no one is going to read it or publish it!

—   DAILY REVIEW. When you lie down in bed to go to sleep, close your eyes and recall your day in reverse order - noticing how you feel about each experience. Start with what happened just before bed and retrace your steps to waking up. If you can, bless or forgive anyone you had a challenging encounter with. This intent to be in right relationship with others causes us to ponder, with a sense of humility, on our own part in the exchange and the lesson we can personally take from it. This practice ensures a much deeper and more restful sleep because we're not trying to resolve everything in our dream state.

— WEEKLY BATH. Being in a body of water helps us to become like the element of water, which when still, becomes reflective. So you may wish to try ending your working week with a long soak to wash off the residue of work until you feel relaxed, soft and available to enjoying your personal time to the fullest. We often enter into a meditative state without even trying when we're in the bath, especially if we bathe alone and have minimal distractions within a sacred space set with candles and soft transcendental music.

— MONTHLY GATHERING. For many years I have taken part in this ancient practice which I can't imagine living without. (This is also the comment made by those I've introduced to it.) It involves sitting in a circle once a month and taking turns to speak about the month you've had. We use a talking stick to ensure everyone gets their designated space to speak, which doesn't always occur in social settings. Sitting in circle is a very powerful process as a circle has no beginning and no end, so this structure creates a vortex of energy which builds as each person takes their turn to speak. The result is that energy is focused, which helps bring to the surface whatever is unresolved in our psyche. I sit in circle with women in my local community at new moon. This gives an opportunity to process the lessons of the previous month, so we can start the coming month feeling clear. The beauty of this practise is that you see aspects of yourself reflected in each person as they speak. This accelerates our getting ofwisdom and enables us to see how universal our human frailties are. Afterwards everyone always feels and looks much lighter and clearer for having shared in a place of true understanding and support. I love this practice so much and feel it is such a great foundation for community building as it supports us as individuals, minimizing conflict in couples and families. I train people the craft of group facilitation to seed sharing circles in their local community via online training courses. (See Resources.)

— ANNUAL ANALYSIS AND GOAL SETTING. Instead of just stating a New Year's resolution as an afterthought at a party after a few wines, consider writing down what you didn't like about the previous year. This may highlight a repeated theme. From there, you can create an action plan with goals to address what didn't work. This practice empowers us with personal accountability. I did an online course which assisted me to do this called, 'Best Year Ever' with Michael Hyatt. I highly recommend going away to do this practice overnight with your partner if in you're in a relationship as a New Year 'couples weekend' as it creates psychological and emotional intimacy when we share our innermost thoughts and feelings about our recent past, followed by our aspirations for the future so you're both, 'on the same page'. Regardless of your relationship status, if you can get away to do this process there's nothing like the perspective of distance to assist you in seeing your life more clearly.

—   SPEAKING WITH A COACH/MENTOR/COUNSELLOR. If you've got a backlog of unresolved experiences, private sessions are a great idea so you're not using your friends, family or work colleagues as sounding boards and wondering why they are reluctant to return your calls! Wise counsel offers fresh insight, enabling us to re-frame experiences so we can be grateful for the lesson and move on. As stated earlier, there are a lot of bad counsellors, just as not all plumbers or shop assistants are well suited to their job. So remember you are well within your rights to interview them for the job. Ask them how they work. For instance, do they just sit there like a lump of wood while you pour your heart out? Or do they offer observations and insights to assist you in shifting old perspectives? What suits one won't suit another, so best find out before you start giving long family histories whether someone is a good fit for you, otherwise you may find you leave feeling   unsupported,   demoralized   and   powerless,   which   is counterproductive.

The more we take the time to focus on digesting our life experiences, the more we support our physical digestion. This is because our tummy is our emotional center, where the archetype of the inner child resides in our energy system. This is why we are more prone to bloating if we have a backlog of unresolved emotional experiences. Poor digestion is exacerbated by our inner child comfort eating or drinking to suppress feeling painful emotions. This is why, when we're upset emotionally it disrupts this function and those who grew up not feeling emotionally safe, supported and held in their family of origin can develop intolerances and digestive problems later in life, due to trauma held within this part of the body. (I explain more about this in my book, 'Creating Sacred Union Within' - see Resources.)

CALL TO ACTION

Choose one of the suggestions above to anchor a habit of regularly processing your experiences. Given many people fear public speaking more than death, sitting in a circle and speaking in front of others is going to be too confronting for those who have never shared their experiences with a private counsellor or healer. So if you haven't sought out private sessions before, start with some private journalling or talking to a counsellor as a starting point. If, however, you have done some journal writing and had one-on-one sessions in the past, do consider taking it up a notch by sitting in a monthly sharing circle. Intuit who of your friends and family might be interested and check out the online training course to start one. For those of you who have recently located, this is a wonderful way to connect with people who are 100% authentic and committed to their personal growth.

DAY 24: HAPPINESS HABIT

THE POWER OF TOUCH

Touch is the most primal form of love. Without it babies die. It is as necessary to our survival as air, water, food and shelter. In Melbourne, Australia where I live, The Royal Women's Hospital has volunteers who hold, cuddle and tenderly stroke the skin of newborn babies born to drug addicted parents due to the survival necessity of touch. Touch is a universal need. Studies show cats who are regularly stroked after having a surgical procedure recover much faster than those who aren't. So in our soul sick culture with its preoccupation on sexual seduction, innocent touch has become rare for fear of social cues being misinterpreted. If we add to this, the generational conditioning from our ancestors, who lived during the Victorian era (and were decidedly repressed about any form of physical affection) we get a broader understanding of how starved for loving touch many of us are. This is more so in Western cultures who have long prided themselves on their civility. In direct contrast, if you visit a developing country, it is not uncommon for everyone to learn massage as a life skill to exchange amongst their family and friends. In the West, a massage is more often something we pay for as a service from a trained professional.

Even in intimate relationships many couples stop touching each other. One may rebuke the other if they feel the only time they are touched is if it's with the intent to have sex. Touch is a turn-off when loaded with an agenda to get something, rather than to give. This is why the quality of touch is so important. So much is conveyed through our touch. We are sentient beings and we sense intent through the energy and emotion emitted through a single touch. Partners who share a great love, touch each other often, not as a precursor to sex, but to express support, understanding, tenderness, play or to help one another relax. When the touch dies, the quality of relating hardens and the likelihood of conflict escalates, impairing the ability to reach out and touch each other. Lovemaking (as opposed to carnal fornication) is borne out of heart-based touch, first and foremost - this is why in Tantra the emphasis is on connecting in the heart.

Regardless of how polished our external veneers may become as adults, we each still have a small child within us who thrives on hugs. For example, yesterday I visited my neighbors and their two young kids, (aged one and three) rushed over and hugged me. I haven't spent loads of time with them which made their openness to express their big hearts in little bodies even more moving.

The power of a hug was understood by a young man here in Sydney, Australia in 2004 who, using the pseudonym, 'Juan Mann' started a free hugs campaign. He simply stood with a sign that said 'Free Hugs' every day in the heart of downtown Sydney. Here is a video of him, which is a tear jerker as it shows how so many of us are afraid of love because loving touch has become such an unfamiliar act in our society. It does, however illustrate how the simple gift of a hug can be a huge act of heart-based activism. (Note: There seems to be some controversy about the band who made the clip so you may want to visit Juan Mann's website listed below if you want to support him rather than buying t-shirts via the band which are advertised during the clip.)

https://www.youtube.com/watch?v=vr3x_RRJdd4

CALL TO ACTION

So today you're going to reach out and touch somebody. Notice if that elicits a fearful response, as this signals you need this more than ever! Have a look at the ideas below and choose one to do today and consider how you can incorporate some of the other suggestions into your life.

WAYS TO REACH OUT AND TOUCH SOMEONE

- Put a supportive hand on the shoulder of your child, friend or colleague.
- Stroke your partner's head or your child's hair.
- Put your hand on the back of someone's heart who feels overwhelmed or anxious.
- Offer to give or exchange a foot or head massage (I give rose petal foot baths with warmed milk, where I drizzle honey on their toes, exfoliating them by giving them a foot massage with a coconut scrub and then anoint their feet with rose oil and kiss them. Always well received!)
- Brush or plait someone's hair with tenderness.
- Stroke and pat your pets often.
- Dare to ask someone if they'd like a hug.
- Visit Juan Mann's website for info on how to start your own local Free Hugs Campaign: http://www.juanmann.com/p/about-free-hugs.html

- On Valentine's Day you may wish to go hold a 'FREE HUGS' sign in your lunch hour for those who could use one.

WAYS TO INCREASE LOVING TOUCH FOR YOURSELF

So too, in our duty of care to ourselves, we need to ensure we receive enough loving touch in our lives on a regular basis if we are to feel truly happy.

- Self-pleasure yourself with loving touch rather than merely as a stress release.
- Swap a massage with a friend or book a massage with a professional once a month.
- Walk barefoot where possible and touch the natural world with your hands.

DAY 25: HAPPINESS HABIT

FOCUS ON THE POSITIVE IN ANY SITUATION

I had a friend say to me that depressed people often have a more accurate perception of reality. I do agree that a lot of depressed people often have quite a firm handle on reality - their downfall is that they tend to fixate on the problems as they exist, rather than focusing on exploring possibilities which require imaginative thinking. So it is true that if we look at life from a purely rational viewpoint, we will probably feel depressed. This is because the rational mind can only comprehend the surface level of reality, the provable facts which are immediately apparent. What it can't perceive are the underlying truths, the greater meaning, which expand our understanding of reality into something inspiring. For when we open our minds to contemplate the BIG PICTURE (the infinite possibilities beyond our comprehension), we let the light of expanded consciousness in to inspire our minds to grow.

Seeing life through a purely rational filter limits us to only a fragment of the whole truth. From this perspective we can feel isolated and alone, which tends to generate fears that we won't get our needs met. From this fearful viewpoint, we often create conflict with those around us. Such a fear-based reality keeps us creating on a negative time track, making small choices to maintain safety, which limits possibilities and becomes a self-fulfilling prophecy of negative expectations.

Like the song, '*Accentuate the Positive*' from the Rogers and Hammerstein musical, '*South Pacific*', if we orient our focus to the blessings we can see in our current situation, we shift gears into a positive time track, increasing the chance of a more positive outcome. This is not the rhetoric of a cock-eyed optimist, a 'Pollyanna' who refuses to see the shadow in the world. The shadow side of life is necessary. It is a great teacher which teaches us what not to do and inspires us to make different choices. For it is often when things don't go according to plan, we learn our greatest lessons. So if we want to transcend depressive tendencies, we need to befriend the chaos - the unknown, by focusing on what it could be showing us, that is ultimately for our benefit.

If we hold a believe that the world is unfair, our own limited thinking will prevent us from seeing the potential gifts in a situation. Whereas, if we entertain the possibility that the benevolent universe is giving us an opportunity for greater understanding and growth in every moment, we have more chance of seeing it from that perspective and elevating our energy field. This lightness of being then attracts people, solutions and serendipitous opportunities that resonate at a similar frequency to our 'attitude of gratitude'!

Here is a famous Chinese parable which teaches us to not judge a situation as negative or positive because in itself, it is only a part of the story. Only time reveals the true fate.

THE PARABLE OF THE LOST HORSE

In a small village near the northern Chinese border lived a wise man well versed in the practices of Taoism. One day his mare wandered off and failed to return. His neighbors, rallied round him and said how sorry they were for his loss.

The man simply replied, 'It is what it is.'

A few months passed and his mare returned, and following her was a very fine stallion. Again, the local villagers came to visit, congratulating the man on his fine fortune.

Again the man replied, 'It is what it is.'

One day the man's son was riding the stallion and he was thrown off, breaking his hip. Again the neighbors lamented the fate of the young man and offered their condolences.

To which man replied, 'It is what it is'.

Soon after a war broke out and all the young men were conscripted to fight to protect the border. The man's son was considered too injured to fight so he remained at home. All the other young men lost their lives. The man's son was the only man of his generation in the village to survive.

This story reminds me of the practice the author, Marianne Williamson suggested to her readers in the 1980's when AIDS was a huge health threat in the West. She encouraged those diagnosed positive with HIV to write a journal entry every day to their disease. Understandably, the majority started off negatively, feeling resentful and verbally abusing their disease for interrupting their plans and confronting them with fears and uncertainty. However, over time a change would occur and they would start to acknowledge all the the positive changes they had made in their lives as a result of living with the disease. Ultimately, many would end up coming to a place of grace where they felt grateful for the disease having catalysed a huge shift in their priorities, so their lives were congruent with their deepest truth. It is said contemplating death is the most powerful way to learn how to honor the gift of life.

CALL TO ACTION

Today you're going to identify a situation in your life which is causing you pain, then write down all the things this situation has taught you, including all the positive changes it has catalyzed in your life. Do this until you can bless this situation and those involved, as this will help you take your personal power back and usher in a more graceful perspective.

DAY 26: HAPPINESS HABIT

ALLOW YOURSELF TO REST AND RELAX

Given our society's technological advances we can find we treat ourselves like machines, with two switches, 'ON' (working / parenting / serving others) and 'OFF' (sleeping). So if we don't structure in quality rest and relaxation time, we fry our nerves and end up waking up like the anxious white rabbit from *'Alice in Wonderland'*, convinced there isn't enough time to get everything done.

Whenever we're focused on time, which is a linear man-made construct, we're in our mind - not our hearts. The heart is the central energy center, so it remains the place of true power where our innate essence emanates. So whilst we need be mindful of the time, if we are to be organized and honor our commitments, if we become obsessed with time, we end up feeling like a rat on a wheel racing against the clock from the moment we wake til the moment we drop.

If done as a habitual way of living, this time obsessed mania leads to a state of complete nervous exhaustion. This can result in chronic fatigue where one's adrenals are so depleted that we can't find the energy to get out of bed or a nervous breakdown where one is so overwrought that emotionally they crack under the strain. Either way, this way of being is not sustainable. So if you recognize the tell-tale signs, take steps to structure in compulsory times to rest. Otherwise we risk becoming more machine than human, like the character, Darth Vader from 'Star Wars' - disconnected from our hearts, with our shadow side calling the shots. When we persist in pushing ourselves past what is constructive, we also become increasingly inefficient, causing costly errors in judgement.

NOURISH YOUR NERVOUS SYSTEM

If we find we are operating in a prolonged state of anxiety, taking the mineral, magnesium every day is a wonderful way to support our nervous system. Most of our soils are now depleted in magnesium, so even if we eat foods considered high in magnesium, chances are we're probably deficient. Certain yoga poses nourish the nervous system, such as 'downward dog' as does shaking all over to rhythmic music, which helps the body release trauma stored within the cells.

THE COMPULSIVE DO-ERS

If we grew up in a family dynamic where we only felt truly seen and affirmed when we were doing something helpful or achieving something special then it is understandable that we anchor 'doing' as a way of gaining love and acceptance. If this is anchored deep in our sub-conscious, we may find it virtually impossible to stop and rest even when we're feeling exhausted.

Similarly, a lot of people grew up in households with unconscious group dynamics where one was either the scapegoat or the bully and so one felt pressured to 'pick a side'. As children in this kind of an environment our nervous system is constantly in a state of preparedness for fight or flight. This can lead to running on anxiety as adults, who never feel deeply safe enough to truly relax. If you recognize yourself in either of these ways - befriend magnesium on a daily basis and try kundalini yogic practices to support your nervous system. In the Resources section I have a 'Chakra Workout' CD with kundalini practices you can do at home or check out a local kundalini yoga or dance class.

THE IMPORTANCE OF DOWN TIME

If we don't give ourselves regular 'down time' it is only a matter of time till we manifest illness or depression to stop, so our body and nervous system can replenish. Like the saying, 'The bigger they are, the harder they fall! if our ego persists in not honoring the needs of our body and all its intricate systems, we will short circuit and break down.

Balance is inevitable, as it is one of the natural laws within our universe. So if we don't exercise balance, it will be created for us. For example, when we can't stop - for fear of not getting everything done, we are manic in our energy polarity. Eventually the pendulum will swing to the opposite polarity and we will fall into the opposite state of depression. Alternatively, we may neglect our body's need for rest in our desire to achieve and be productive, then inevitably become so run down we are more susceptible to the airborne viruses and bacterial germs constantly around us.

One does not need to be diagnosed 'bi-polar' to observe this pendulum of behavior swinging in their own lives. We all have kundalini (life force energy) running through the sub-stations along our central nervous cord in our spines. This nervous energy is the body's own electrical current. If this energy is not grounded it becomes dangerous, just like electricity - resulting in violent storms, such as emotional, mental and physical outbursts. Stimulants like coffee, sugar and pseudoephedrine spike our energy even more, making us even more erratic. So to ensure our behaviour is safe, both for ourselves and others, we need to make a concerted effort to stay as grounded as possible. The more grounded we are, the slower our heart rate and the more centered, calm and content we feel. When we are grounded (in our bodies, embodying the Earth element) we are more likely to get a better night's sleep, which ensures we're less erratic.

CALL TO ACTION

Today you're going to identify at least one way you can support your nervous system and put it into action. As always, try and incorporate more of the suggestions below into your daily life.

HOW TO STAY GROUNDED AND UNWIND AN OVERACTIVE (ANXIOUS) MIND

- Connect to the Earth! I like to start every morning with the 'Tree of Life' meditation followed by some yoga. This meditation evolved from numerous traditions and simply involves using creative visualization to energetically connect to the Earth by sending energetic roots down to the center of Mother Earth from the base of your spine. I've recorded this as an MP3 if you find it easier to have a guided meditation to assist you to visualize. (See Resources.)

    - Walk barefoot as much as possible to ensure the major kidney meridian, which is the foundation for our immune system is connected to the Earth. This strengthens our immune system. For more info on this read the book, 'Earthing' by Clinton Ober.

    - Eat protein regularly and avoid processed foods high in sugar, caffeine, energy stimulants like guarana and pharmaceuticals containing pseudoephedrine.

    - Energize and nurture your body regularly with exercise, self- pleasure, lovemaking and massages.

    - Read a book that is not work-related, such as poetry or fiction.

    - Look at art.

    - Unplug from technology.

    - Have a bath.

    - Go for a walk (in nature if possible).

    - Do something creative that isn't work-related.

−Guided Meditation (rather than trying to completely silence the mind when you're hyped up, use this technique to give the mind a focus, making it easier to calm down).

−Schedule regular mental health days by switching off completely from technology which can keep our minds in a constant state of being 'on'. You may wish to make Sundays your tech-free day to help you to recharge and reboot.

DAY 27: HAPPINESS HABIT

EXPRESS YOUR LOVE IN CREATIVE WAYS

Love is a state of being. It is our essence. Love is the force of all creation that unifies opposites, a phenomena which generates new life. At its very core, love is creative. So the more creative thought we apply to express our love, the more love we generate - for ourselves and the recipient. The giving and sharing of love heals and restores. It creates opportunities and possibilities for growth. It affirms life and the simple truth that we are all connected as one collective consciousness.

There are many forms of love and we need all types of love if we are to thrive. So despairing you cannot express all the love inside you because you don't have a partner limits who you are as a loving being. The ancient Greeks coined four types of love:

AGAPE: Love of all fellow human beings. To fill this chamber in our heart we perform benevolent acts of kindness towards others and extend understanding and acceptance beyond judgment.

PHILEO: This is the love of platonic friendship. Spending time to listen to and extend care to those with whom we share a kinship and resonance with.

STORGE: This is the unconditional love we feel with those we share a familiar bond with. These may be family members or the family we choose - our soul clan.

EROS: This is what we feel when passionate and intense romantic love is ignited and fuelled by a desire to express our erotic desires.

The ancient Greek did not include SELF LOVE which I feel is the foundation of all love, for without this, no other love can flourish. For when this love dwindles, we generate less to share in the previous four ways.

GENERATE LOVE BY GIVING LOVE

When we focus on how we can share and show our love, the very intent fills us with feelings of love and increases our urge to express it. This is why giving is such a high. How much of a high, depends upon how much creative thought and effort we put into it. We see this illustrated by the number of women who enquire, 'How did he propose?' in response to someone announcing their wedding engagement. It is because they want to experience the thrill of hearing the creative lengths to which one has gone to express their love. For each act of love inspires the heart anew and validates the notion that true love exists.

LOVE IS NOT AFRAID TO RISK LOOKING LIKE A FOOL

The following is an excerpt from my book, *'Creating Sacred Union in Partnerships'* (in resources).

'It takes creativity to express one's romantic heart; creative thought to hatch the idea and then ingenuity, skill and daring to pull it off. To be creative, one must enter a space where they are at one with the creative source of all life...the animating presence of the divine! So the more creative you are with your date nights, birthday ideas, unexpected surprises on a Friday night, the more your partner will be moved to merge with you, and adore and worship you as Divine!

This is why women develop crushes on the same heartthrobs that feature in numerous romantic comedies, as they repeatedly fulfill fantasies of a man who will go to great lengths to show their beloved the enormity of their feelings. It is this willingness to express their heart, their true essence that will melt the heart of a woman.

One lovely example I recall of a man of average looks and a low income enchanting a house full of women was when I was in college. He was the partner of one of my housemates. He arrived at the front of our house on the morning of her birthday with an eight foot birthday card he had made from plywood and painted! It wasn't expensive, it wasn't even painted that well, but it was larger than life, it was ridiculous and it was a statement to the world that he loved her and he didn't care who knew. It filled all five of us young women with joy, having proof that loving men existed - not to mention a memory we'll never forget. What this delightful young man demonstrated was a comedic device known as exaggeration - doing something deliberately larger than expected to the point of ridiculousness. This silliness appeals to the magical child within, lightening our spirits with the fifth element, Spirit - the element of surprise.

'Comedy is when you expect something to break and it bends'
W.C. Fields

In fact, given that most women want a partner who will risk looking like a fool for love - I recommend seeking inspiration from the world of comedy for those seeking to woo their partner with romantic gestures. (Again this is why romantic comedies are bankable commodities with the female demographic.) This is because this genre evokes the archetypal fool, one who expresses all of their selves without any self-conscious fears about what other people think. Only a man who truly knows and is comfortable with himself can do this. This is essentially a man bearing his soul, his innocence which is the exact opposite of what men in the patriarchal era were conditioned to express.'

If you feel cynical about romantic love, watch some of the wedding proposal flash mobs on You Tube.

LOVE IS OUR LEGACY

It is the degree to which we love that people will remember us by. A few years ago my friend, Merle died at sixty-seven suddenly from a stroke. This is a woman who was still wearing platform shoes to work! At her funeral the most memorable part was when two of her grandsons stood before the congregation and showed us the 'Tickle Chart' they had made illustrating the thirteen stages of tickling their Nana used to do to them.

Today is an opportunity to create your legacy - don't waste it focusing on love lost, unrequited love or love turned sour. Instead, look to how you can be that force of regenerative love that heals and uplifts all. Bless Merle and all the great teachers of this truth, the big hearts who show us how to love.

The mind is often quick, decisive and quick to dismiss those who operate from their hearts. However those who at first appear foolish, get the last laugh when their innocent agenda to simply love, melts the heart of the biggest cynic. This is true of my partner, who constantly humbles me with his purity of heart. Some time ago he broke one of my favorite necklaces that I had loved for many years. It was not expensive, it did not contain precious or semi- precious jewels, but I loved it for its color and creativity. I expressed my disappointment then accepted I could no longer wear it, but I couldn't bring myself to throw it away. On Valentine's Day he presented me with it. He had spent hours figuring out a way to fix it with his own hands. This dedication to make something right is a beautiful act of love. Given how commercial Valentine's Day has become I felt it important to share this story so one need not make a political statement against Valentine's Day by becoming miserly. Rather, let it inspire us to truly give of ourselves - regardless of the occasion. Love doesn't have to be fancy or expensive...it simply has to be pure in its motive. To me, that is the essence of the Tantric path of wisdom - finding an infinite number of ways to express your true heart's appreciation of the divine made manifest.

DAY 28: HAPPINESS HABIT

RECONNECT AND PRACTICE ONENESS

Just as life is infinite, there are an infinite number of ways we can merge with and feel 'at one' with the source of all life. So quibbling over which path is the 'right' way is redundant and the fastest way to get caught up in the illusions of the mind. Illusions which prevent us from hearing the quieter sensations of our heart, where all truth resides. When we take our awareness into our heart, we are connected to all of existence. This is because the one pulsating rhythm of life is within every living thing. (If your mind rebukes the notion we are one, I highly recommend watching the film, '*I Am*' by Tom Shadyac, in which they perform scientific tests, based on the work of the heartmath institute to prove this theory.)

When we perceive and act from this unified perception we treat others as reflections of the one sacred essence, expressing itself through different forms. Life also becomes easier and more graceful when we view each other from heart-centered oneness, as others sense our motivation is pure, and to benefit all and they respond accordingly.

Only seven percent of our communication is verbal with ninety-three percent being non-verbal. Scientific studies concluded the non-verbal component was made up of body language (fifty- five percent) and our tone of voice (thirty-eight percent). However, these studies don't account for the energetic transmission which occurs when we encounter someone's energy field, colloquially referred to as their 'vibe'. The more evolved and sensitive we become, the more we base our communication on what we perceive through our subtle senses. So if we clad ourselves in psychic armor, anticipating a battle with others, we will more than likely experience that as the probable outcome.

I am reminded of the parable of the doe and the bear...a bear has a thorn in his paw and is inciting terror amongst all the other mountain-dwelling animals with his growls. Only the innocent doe can approach him to find out what the problem is, as the young doe doesn't react to the outward behavior, but instead asks his inner self, 'What ails you?'

This lesson is handy to remember if ever you find yourself face-to-face with someone who is enraged - be it your partner, a child throwing a tantrum or even a potential predator. If you can resist being ruled by fear in that instance and breathe into your heart to sincerely enquire, 'What is the source of your pain and frustration?' Such a response is unexpected for the mind and will cause them to falter, giving you the opportunity to help them come back to their heart and remember their humanity by expressing the sadness beneath the rage. This is the heroic response to which the true hero aspires, standing strong in who we are, when faced with an enemy. Neither cowering or attacking but seeking greater understanding from a place of genuine compassion for a fellow soul. Rather than inflame the polarity of victim and aggressor, a genuine heart concern will help dissipate the inflammatory energy by directly addressing the cause rather than reacting to the symptom.

CALL TO ACTION

Today you are going to practice responding to whatever life throws at you from the centeredness of the heart, rather than judgement and fear of the mind.

QUICK WAYS TO RECONNECT WITH YOUR HEART

—   BREATHING - inhaling deeply energizes the lungs, supplying more blood to the physical heart. This helps brings our conscious awareness from focusing on thoughts to experiencing our feelings. This makes us available to the present moment rather than being stuck in the heads, focusing on thoughts relevant to the past or the future.

—   PUT YOUR HAND ON YOUR HEART - this helps re-focus our awareness and attention to be heart-centered. If you feel distressed, gently pat, rub or self-massage the center of your chest.

—   ASK, 'WHAT WOULD LOVE DO?' This helps disarm our mental, emotional and energetic bodies, making us more open to reconciliatory action, rather than engaging in defensive behavior.

To help you to stay heart-centered throughout your day, I recommend starting your day with a practice.

START YOUR DAY BY RECONNECTING

As I've stated previously, there's any number of ways to do this, so if you find one that works for you - stick to it. If not, go to a Tai Chi, Qi Gong or Yoga class or watch an instructional video on You Tube. Here are the practices I've found helpful which you may like to try:

ACTIVE MEDITATION PRACTICES. Meditation is any practice that gets us out of our mind so we are one hundred percent in the moment - athletes call this, 'the zone'. When we have an active mind, it often takes an active meditation to express all of our unexpressed energy before we can enter into a state of stillness. There are a number of ways to do this including:

- Shaking your body to rhythmic music.
- Free-form dancing, especially to music that takes you up the chakras.
- Devotional chanting.
- Going for a run in nature.

SEMI-ACTIVE MEDITATION PRACTICES. These are gentle activities which engage the mind with a focus of sacred oneness, such as:

- Walking in nature with the intent of noticing beauty.
  - Repeating an incantation, such as 'All is One'.
  - Coloring in a mandala.
  - Yin yoga (spending 5 mins in each pose and deepening one's surrender).

PASSIVE MEDITATION PRACTICES. These are activities which slow down our heart rate and brainwave activity, enabling us to move into altered states of consciousness. Activities such as:

- Sitting with the eyes closed while focusing on the breath entering and leaving the body.
- Sitting with eyes closed focusing on a mantra, such as the word, 'peace' on both the in breath and out breath.
- Silent meditation.
- Guided meditation (great to do in the bath).
- Gazing into a candle flame, an open fire or up at the stars or clouds.
- Gazing at a vast expanse, such as the ocean or a valley.

—Bringing oneself into a heightened state of awareness in the present moment through observing the sounds, smells, sights and sensations within and without.

INVOCATION. Another helpful tip to remain heart-centered is to ask each day that you be a vessel to serve highest wisdom. Since energy follows intention, this helps us to anchor our Soul as the bus driver for the day, rather than our ego.

BONUS HAPPINESS HABIT

EXERCISE !

I decided to add this one in as I've personally noticed a HUGE difference in my own daily happiness levels from being regularly active, compared to the times when I haven't, and felt more prone to depressive feelings.

Like many people in our IT driven world, I have a sedentary job, sitting in front of a computer, writing. I love what I do, but it means I have to ensure I make an effort to move my body by setting aside time every day to exercise.

Exercise has many benefits for me personally.

- It aids my digestion and circulation so I don't feel cold and bloated, which helps me to feel happier in my body.
- It moves stagnant emotional energy so it gives me a way of discharging frustration so I feel buoyant from the physical release.
- It improves my fitness and strength, so I feel better equipped to deal with whatever task is at hand with more confidence.
- I am leaner when I exercise regularly and this helps me feel energized and increases my libido.

Exercise has also been proven to help those diagnosed with depression. In a study published in 'Medicine and Science in Sports and Exercise' forty people who had been clinically diagnosed, but were not taking anti-depressant medication were divided into two groups. One group rested for thirty minutes and the others walked on a treadmill. Afterwards both groups were asked to complete surveys. Both groups reported fewer negative feelings, such as tension, depression, anger or fatigue, but only those who exercised reported feeling positive feelings.

Another study, by John Ratey, M.D., author of 'Spark: The Revolutionary New Science of Exercise and the Brain' found that just twenty minutes of exercise produces subtle feelings of well-being for up to twelve hours afterwards. Science also cites the reasons for this; serotonin (the feel good neurochemical) is released, and dopamine levels rise. (Dopamine is the neurotransmitter which controls our pleasure centers). Dopamine also helps us be pro-active and feel less addictive according to 'Psychology Today'

So, if you're not already doing some kind of daily exercise, explore your options. The mind may offer a litany of excuses, such as 'I hate gyms', 'I don't have the time' or 'I have a bad back'. This is the saboteur who resists change. The stronger the saboteur, the more support you will need to enlist to transcend those limiting thoughts.

If the excuse is, 'I hate gyms' Google groups that get together in a local park, ask a friend to go on regular walks in nature or check out local dance classes. If the excuse is, 'I don't have time' look at how you can maximise the time you have by always taking the stairs, have meetings while walking on a treadmill via Skype or doing things with your kids on weekends that will get you moving like rollerskating or bike riding. If the excuse is, 'I have a bad back', check out your local swimming pool for water based exercise options. In other words, don't let your defeatist self have the final word.

Personally, I found I needed to pay a membership to a health club to ensure I hauled ass off the couch because I can't stand the idea of wasting money. I've also found one that offers a thirty minute circuit which appeals to my saboteur who wouldn't always find the time for a walk.

I also recommend building exercise into your existing routine. For example, I used to drop my daughter at school then head straight to the gym then go home, shower and start work. Like many folk, I found that if I left exercising until the afternoon, when our shadows look larger, the chance of me not going increased the later it got. Many people find it helpful to exercise before going to work. This is harder if you have to get kids off to school, however I have known some mums who would get up before their kids to exercise.

If your saboteur is particularly strong, find a way to be accountable. Just as I pay a membership, you may prefer to have a trainer or a friend who you meet with and don't want to let down. Starting is always hardest part, but it gets easier and easier to maintain once you start reaping the benefits. When it becomes a habit if you miss a day, you don't feel as good which affirms what a great habit it is to maintain.

CALL TO ACTION

Today, do something to move your body. Go for a walk outdoors or if the weather is inhospitable, go for a swim in a heated pool after work or with your kids after school. If you're time poor, put on one of your favorite tracks and have a dance in your lounge room before heading out the door or call a friend to have a game of tennis or kick a ball round a soccer field with your kids. Think of friends who might be interested in joining you for a regular walk, which is a great chance to catch up with each other or check out local sports teams, leisure centers or health clubs.

CONGRATULATIONS!

Well done on making it through your 28 challenges to create a happier life! I sincerely hope you feel happier for having participated in this experience with me.

You may wish to return as an annual challenge every Autumn / Fall when the days start to get grey, as inspiration you to keep your spirits bright.

Alternatively, you may feel to dip into it as needed by asking the book, 'What insight do I most need from this today?' Then open it up randomly on a page and read what it says. (This is an ancient Celtic tradition, consulting a book as an oracle.)

I do hope you've found the suggestions both practical and applicable to your life and incorporate them into your daily life, moving forwards, as it is in the doing rather than in the knowing, that we find the essence of any teachings.

Thank-you again for supporting this project to help girls and women rebuilding their lives after being sold (often as children) into a life of sexual slavery. Please consider gifting this book to others who you think would find it helpful, either as a paperback or ebook for occasions such as birthdays or Christmas to help a worthy cause. To stay in touch and get the latest news about my upcoming events: Join my free eclub: http://www.starofishtar.com/

May your days be sunny and bright.

Blessings,
Tanishka

RESOURCES

MEDITATIONS

CD / MP3 tracks of my morning meditation practices from my album, 'The Chakra Workout':

http://www.starofishtar.com/meditation-mp3/

APP

Here's the link for my Moon Woman app: http://www.starofishtar.com/moon-woman-mobile-app/

BOOKS

The following titles are available as paperbacks or ebooks at: http://www.starofishtar.com/product-category/books/

'The Inner Goddess Makeover' 'Creating Sacred Union Within' 'Creating Sacred Union in Partnerships'

COURSES

Red Tent Sisterhood Circles Facilitator Online Training Course:

http://www.starofishtar.com/courses/red-tent-online-course-for- women/

Brotherhood Lodge Men's Circles Facilitator Online Training Course:

http://menscirclefacilitatortrainingcourse.gr8.com/

Sacred Union For Singles and Couples Online Course:

http://taniskasacredunioncourse.gr8.com/

FILMS

'Happy' http://www.thehappymovie.com/ 'I Am'
http://www.iamthedoc.com/

Made in the USA
Lexington, KY
27 February 2018